# JOURNEY TO UNITY

## THE PATH TO A NEW AMERICAN MAJORITY

### BY GARRY HARPER, M.Th.S.

1

# PREFACE

The nation is divided as never before except, perhaps, during the Civil War. It was then that politicians raised armies to defend two widely divergent visions of America. Each side cloaked their ambitions in versions of morality knowing that only one plan would survive. They also knew that the losing side would end up holding the mantle of "immorality." During that horrible time over 3 million men went to war and more than 600,000 lost their lives.

Thankfully no shots have been fired in this current conflict of ideas. Still, without a shot being fired, millions of ordinary citizens litter our political battlefields in anguish and despair. They have been wounded by a system that corrupts clarity of mind and seems to always doom one side or the other to a permanent state of irrelevance. The intellectual foundation of the nation has been abandoned for the most part because a reasoned argument wouldn't fit into the evening news and too few people would watch or listen even if it did.

Congressional arguments are sustained by stylish language steeped in emotional symbolism rather than logical substance. Both sides "feel" strongly about the righteousness of their position. Emotions run high especially among the core groups within both major political parties.

The head to head debates between President Lincoln and Senator Steven Douglas featured two men who spent hours facing each other without a journalist to moderate their debate or influence the direction of their arguments. In today's debates a very small minority of Americans tune in to see and hear emotion-filled tirades between professional politicians who rarely actually answer a question but never fail to hit their "talking points." Amazingly each side has become an expert in describing nothing but the opposing view in less than flattering ways. Neither side bothers to intellectually defend their own position because they have become aware of the fact that it is conflicts rather than solutions that drives television ratings.

Over the past 60 years America has learned a new way to make decisions – its mind not burdened by fact, logic or principle. Instead, images of health, happiness and beauty move the populace in the direction of whiter teeth, suppler skin and fashionable dress. News organizations, once the lifeline of American understanding, limit information flow to snippets of sensational sound bites that drive ratings rather than rational thought. Worse, the media itself has taken sides in the great debates using the power of propaganda to push one agenda or another.

This kind of emotion without reason has also infected modern churches. Whereas preachers of the 19th Century labored before a people nearly as familiar with Scripture as themselves, today's congregations would be none the wiser if sermons were based on Hollywood scripts. It is not surprising that the largest churches in America are little more than entertaining social clubs with inspiring musical performances followed by the commercial messages of aspiring entrepreneurial preachers. Inspiration, lest it fade, is made available like a narcotic in the form of CD's and videos available through money-changers in the church foyer.

Throughout this transformation life has imitated art to the point that art *is* life. Americans paint the portrait of their lives on a whitewashed canvass colored by their constant quest to be unique – though all the while they are simply conforming to the advertising aims of 5th Avenue ad agencies.

The question is can any nation advance intellectually and spiritually where resistance to intellectual pursuits is so rampant. Imagine a world where Star Trek's aliens, "The Borg," come to assimilate the depth and breadth of America's intellect. What would it gain beyond the cinematography of Avatar?

An intellectual journey makes up the following chapters. The fine line between the intellect and the spirit of man will often seem to disappear. This is only appropriate given the spiritual nature of humanity. That nature becomes most evident when someone dies. At death there seems to be nothing left but a corpse. What once was is no longer. The mind and essence is gone but we that remain do have memories representing a legacy in words, images and artifacts the deceased left behind. People really do leave something of themselves behind and we all recognize those things as "spiritual." If all of America died in this moment, what would that legacy be?

This journey is also individual. The path taken by this nation as a whole can be seen in trends but the fact is every individual citizen is unique and driven by personal dreams or ambitions. This work is intended to foster personal discovery in the areas of theology, economics, religion and politics. It is not about reading writing and arithmetic. It is about those things that speak into a person's soul and, ultimately, motivate action.

As you read keep in mind this underlying proposition: Human individuals develop a theology – some might call this a "life-view" – before entering into any form of social organization. That theology will drive an individual's social views and opinions first in economics and together with theology will drive political and religious action.

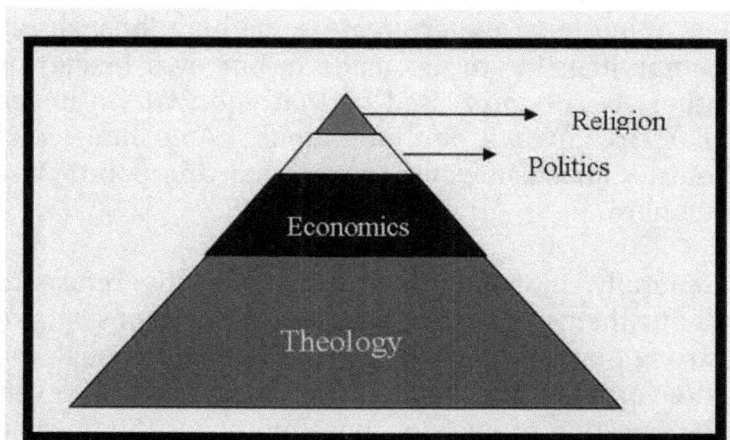

# PART ONE

## IS THERE A GOD; IS A GOD THERE; or perhaps THERE, A GOD IS

Who can presume to add anything to the debate of God? So much has already been written; so much spoken in his or her stead. For example the need, in humanity's mind, to provide a sexual orientation for god is evidence that who or whatever he/she may be, our mind must either create something intrinsically comprehensible to us (made in our own image) or otherwise be impressed by that god with an image that circumvents our limitations. Any intellectual journey must, however, have a starting point. Why not here?

Generally, individual humans steadfastly refuse to define themselves as creatures. The sense of self is so strong that all things "other" are defined through the filter of one's own reality. Sooner or later, however, the question of one's purpose motivates the journey for meaning. While amusing to consider whether it was the chicken or egg which first emerged on earth's scene it might be more useful first to consider whether God preceded man or man, of necessity, invented God or gods as the case may be.

It was Anselm, Archbishop of Canterbury, who said, "God is that beyond which nothing greater can be conceived." In so saying, he put the rub where it would hurt the most – squarely on the limitation of mankind itself. God had to be beyond mankind's ability to conceive anything greater. Some might argue that there is no limit to mankind's imagination. Once imagined nearly anything can be made. And yet, mankind is limited to that which is already here.

As of yet nothing that man has created has come from anything other than that which already existed. Still, one may argue that it is only a matter of time before mankind is able to make something out of nothing. History has shown there is very little that mankind cannot achieve given enough time. But time, as Einstein so aptly proved, is itself a part of creation as we know it. Even *time* is something that is already "here" as part of the time-space continuum.

It is within the space-time continuum that mankind's limitation is most evident. Death overtakes all that has ever been known. Even stars die. Matter is converted to energy and energy back to matter. Within that cycle, time marches forever in a single direction – forward. Moving backward in time, while theoretically possible (so say some theoretical physicists) is admittedly unlikely. If it were possible, someone from our future would have already done so.

Similarly limited is the human body itself. Discoveries have lengthened life spans – even improved the quality of life itself – but the body does have its limitations. Some are stronger and faster than others but, again, history shows the law of diminishing returns as it relates to human endurance. World or Olympic records are admittedly broken on a somewhat regular basis. But while tenths or hundredths of a second can be shaved from the 100 meter run, the pace of improvement is subject to the same death march of time. It is not as though a single human can continuously beat the previous record ad infinitum.

Here, again, one sees a dramatic limitation of humanity. It is not proper, in considering whether it was man or a god who first became "real" unless it becomes a singular man or woman to whom the comparison is judged. If mankind created God or the gods, which man or woman was it that did so? However unfair that might seem – to force a single human to bear the weight of all creation – it must be so because of humanity's insistence on a single person's unique and sovereign identity. On the one hand, a person will insist that he or she is uniquely in charge of themselves. On the other, no single person can accurately claim to have brought about all of the reality that is here.

Those who steadfastly insist that collective humanity is its own judge and jury point to mankind's self determination (the spirit of the individual) and say, "See there? Humanity as a whole determines what is right and wrong within a voluntary society of mankind." To this it must be said that there has been no consistency of societal judgment since time immemorial. Wars, wars and more wars put this argument to rest. Those who stubbornly believe otherwise are humanists in the first degree – that is they act with aforethought to elevate humanity regardless of contrary evidence. Humanism is not a term of derision here but simply one of definition.

The evident reality that *something* existed before mankind (scientists often refer to the primordial soup of life) eliminates mankind from the list of potential creators begging the question of whether or not there is *something* or *someone* out there fitting

Anselm's description of God. If so, humanity must take its proper place among those things either created or induced into existence by something "other" in or even outside of nature. One could properly argue that nature is, after all, either the creation or the emergence of something out of nothing (as humanity understands nothingness).

Is it to God or a god that humanity must inevitably turn? Insofar as humanity seeks meaning on a societal level God or a god must be plausible. But is it a certainty? Society does seek meaning just as it seeks justice. Meaning and justice are either the invention of society as a whole (lack of consistency smashes this theory) or possibly an undeniable expectation somehow resident within the mind of a single individual who then rationalizes meaning and justice in terms that satisfy that person alone.

The "me" generation of the 1960's and 70's was not the first generation to thus find meaning. Anyone remotely versed in human history can see that humans seek recognition first as an individual. That is the foundation upon which Thomas Jefferson penned the words of the Declaration of Independence when he wrote, "We hold these truths to be self-evident, that all men are created equal, that they are endowed by their Creator with certain unalienable Rights, that among these are Life, Liberty and the pursuit of Happiness."

How is it that an expectation that we are all equal (created thus or not) with unalienable rights comes into being? For Jefferson (at least publicly) the endowment came from the Creator of the individual implying at least that the perception is somehow innate within all of us. As wise or prescient as he might have been, even Jefferson was not the first to conceive of that possibility. Is it only a possibility or is it fact? Is there a God? Is a God there?

As it is clearly evident that humanity is nothing if not individual humans, the answer must remain within the individual human being. For those individuals who steadfastly hold to their sovereignty – those humanists who choose to exclusively acknowledge their own being – God or a god may not be a necessity. For those who choose to acknowledge a Creator the decision is equally measured. Each path is an individual decision and each decision is based on one thing only – faith. One either places faith in oneself or in "that beyond which nothing greater can be conceived." So it is only a matter of deciding upon whom one's faith rests most comfortably. It can then be said, "There, is a God."

Henry (Abraham Harold) Maslow's "hierarchy of needs" should be familiar to anyone with a public education but probably is not. In his studies of primate dominance and human sexuality, Maslow chose to study only healthy individuals. From this he produced a seminal work, *Motivation and Personality*, in 1954. He opined that human beings have an ordered pursuit of need fulfillment.

The most common portrayal of this work is a pyramid divided into five sections from the bottom to the top. Human needs are shown prioritized from the most basic and elemental needs (on the bottom of the pyramid) to those needs humans seek to fulfill once each successive level is fundamentally satiated. The most elemental need of humanity was labeled physiological – things like breathing, food, sex, etc. The idea was that once a human being satisfied those needs another set of higher needs would be pursued. The next level was labeled safety. It included things like security of body, employment, resources and so on.

Imagine a couple of humans, a man and a woman, living together in pursuit of those needs Maslow described as most fundamental. Together they attempt to keep breathing, to find or hunt for food and, of course, to meet the most fundamental of social drives – sex.

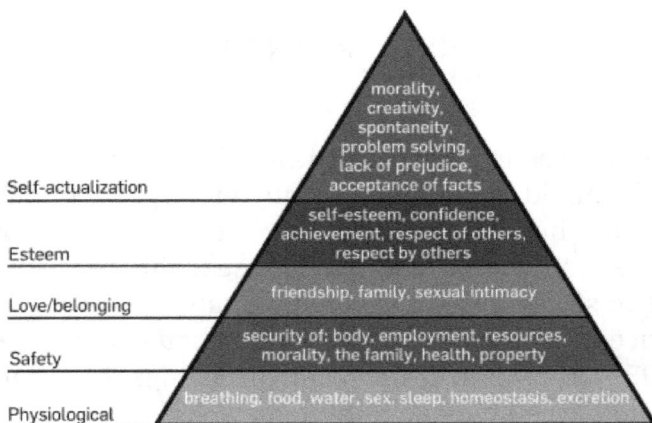

Whether living together as a couple or even singly as individuals these needs would certainly take precedence over those farther up the pyramid. The fact is moving beyond the most basic needs on the lowest level presupposes some form of social intercourse or the foundation of a society.

If Maslow's theory is correct, and many place great faith in its veracity, the next level of human need incorporates some modest level of economic cooperation. Those needs listed as "Safety" needs certainly imply that an economic organization precedes anything that would remotely resemble political organization. Why would that be important? Any society that survives long enough for political organization will first develop a broadly accepted form of economic organization. It becomes the foundation upon which political thought has meaning. When a society fundamentally disagrees on the basis of economic cooperation the political structure will shatter along economic lines.

Americans are in the midst of a societal journey right now. The differences between individual needs and societal needs have pushed well beyond the capacity of political compromise. The political division within America would not be so alarming if the two major parties – Democrat and Republican – were operating under the same economic assumptions. They are not. Each has a significant difference of opinion concerning the appropriate societal economic structure and those opinions are primarily based (acknowledged or not) on where and upon whom the individual places faith. Theology dictates economic organization.

The differences are neither rationally understood nor appropriately communicated. Instead, emotional appeals eclipse genuine understanding and cast a shadow over the Country to a point similar to that of the Civil War period. The Country is in an emotion-laden argument made more severe by the rhetorical devices commonly used in America's media. It does not help matters that both sides are preaching to choirs they have assembled over the years using (sometimes misusing) "texts" from the common "Scripture" of our heritage.

What is that "Scripture?" It is the foundational beliefs (one might just as easily insert the word, "faiths,") that prompted Americans to associate in the first place. "Scripture," in this usage isn't just our founding documents but the underlying presuppositions of social order carried into the "lively experiment" by normal human beings with a common history. During those preceding generations concepts and terms of language had broadly accepted meaning.

Today, American society has almost nothing left of common value insomuch as the two political parties are concerned. Ideas that were once held to be "self-evident" have been pushed into the dustbin of history. It is not uncommon for a society to evolve. Advances in human understanding have certainly shifted the paradigm of more than a few preceding generations. At one time nearly everyone believed the world was flat and lived accordingly. Similarly, human history is full of religious or political ideas that burdened society and even prompted wars.

The shift in viewpoints, represented by the two major political parties, did not occur overnight. Through successive generations – each with societal needs changing much like Maslow's theory – America has emerged from the stages of meeting physiological needs, to safety needs, through the need to love and belong to something of intrinsic value and into the higher echelons Maslow described. Where are we now?

American society, if acting as an individual, would certainly be struggling toward self-actualization. It is that state of being where one seeks meaning and justice. The problem is American society is barely social anymore because those common values and moral judgments that once seemed immoveable have collapsed into something that approaches anarchy in a political context and moral anorexia in terms of social values.

When a society moves away from the two most fundamental foundations of its organization – a common faith and a common economic structure – the political organization will fail. Amidst political failure anarchy almost always asserts itself. One need only look to the Continent of Africa to see the atrocities that follow moral and economic failure.

What then is the truest basis for the economic structure of human society? To get there one must first retrace some concepts from the previous chapter. In short, social organization of humans begins with a commonly held "faith" either in the individual as a sovereign entity whose morality is completely based on self-actualization within or without a social structure or in a Being who, by faith, is believed to be the Source of all things and the mediator of meaning and justice.

Those who place their faith in themselves have the freedom to erect an economy that suits them individually. With that freedom they can enter into social contract with others of like mind or simply enter and exit society at will. Theirs is a world whose moral composition can and often does shift with the prevailing tides of public opinion. Outside of their own opinion there is neither right nor wrong.

The only thing preventing a social structure of these individuals from collapsing into brute force is an economic pact formed through the mutual exchange of value. Using something "valuable" to them they buy or receive goods or services they, as individuals, desire.

Forming a political will among those who place "faith" in themselves is a bit like herding cats. It is only through the rise of a common "religion" that these individuals become trained or coerced into thinking as a political group. Religion, in this context, is nothing more or less than a commonly practiced morality based very loosely on those practices which foster economic gain or personal safety. One could just as easily label this as a philosophy rather than a "religion" but the underpinning of communal action is moral in nature making religion a more suitable description. Members of this "religion" join others of like mind for one singular purpose – personal gain.

It now begins to look as though these self-faith individuals can be arbitrary in their moral values. In fact, as individuals acting in community, values are by definition arbitrary. It would seem that a better description of their behavior is to just use the word "selfish." Since for them morality is completely self-described and mutable (easily changed) that is a great word to describe their behavior.

Americans are frequently accused of "voting their pocket book." This is simply one example of selfish behavior and it is tied to both the religion of self-faith and to the economic structure of pure capitalism that most commonly emerges wherever there is no political structure to act as a check on what would be "normal" human behavior for the self-faith or "selfish" individual.

Without a political structure (and one rarely emerges without economic stress) self-faith individuals enjoy a kind of democratic society where their individual "vote" is exercised through daily economic exchanges. Individuals vote with their dollars or whatever forms of currency the social organization accepts. The most successful individuals accumulate capital or currency while the less successful attempt to either eke out a living or move on to another more promising society. History compels the acknowledgment that unrestricted capitalism accelerates the division between those who have wealth and those who struggle to make a living.

Once the economic democracy is in place, self-faith individuals can and do decide to restrict economic liberty through political organization with a mind toward erecting protections against the tyranny of wealth or the desperations of poverty.

Just so, political organization erupts in societies of self-faith individuals. Individuals organize, often through great personal pains, to establish controls on wealth accumulation. It was so in America during its earliest formation, during the industrial revolution and it is the principle ambition of many Americans today.

What about those who place their "faith" in "that beyond which nothing greater can be conceived? The answer might surprise the objective observer.

When presented with all that is evident in the cosmos, some individuals will choose to place their faith in "that beyond which nothing greater can be conceived." Throughout human history individuals with common predispositions have organized around various "Faiths." Most incorrectly call these religions. It is incorrect because "religion" has more to do with the practice of one's faith than the faith itself.

In this case it is "theology" that best describes that faith. When speaking of God or a multiplicity of gods the subject is theology not religion.

A common statement made by professors to first-year theology students is, "There is no such thing as having no theology…one's theology is either good or bad." Of course the Institution dispensing theological instruction often sees itself as good and all others something less or even bad. The point is that those who place their faith in God should be intellectually honest and spiritually consistent in describing the character of their God.

It would be well here also to explain that those who place their faith in God view those self-faith individuals described in the previous chapter with a jaundiced eye. Placing one's faith in one's self would, to them, be bad theology, even heresy. Herein lays one of the most dangerous elements facing America today. That discussion, however, must be given its space later in this journey. For now the focus must be sustained on those who place their faith in God. Who or what that God is presents more than just a few problems.

While the nation is extremely diverse it is most fitting (and simpler) to focus on the most dominant theology – Christianity. It is this theology that most influences this nation's individuals. However, America's most disturbing divisions have root in the ignorance of Christian theology within and without its adherents.

No writer can completely escape the error of oversimplification when it comes to describing a given theology. Still, America deserves an honest, if not perfectly skilled, assessment of the Christian theology that motivates millions of Americans to economic and political action. The underlying proposition in that statement is that theology actually does motivate economic and political behavior. The proof follows.

The most important thing to do at this moment is to set aside any preconceptions about "Religious Christianity" in America. As stated before, religion is about practices and the subject here is theology. Christian theology is amazingly consistent given the fractious nature of the various denominations of Christianity within America. Those divisions are mainly based on practice rather than theology. In the main, Christianity's theology – its concept of God and man's place in the cosmos – is a shared theology with only minor differences.

In varying degrees Christians support their ideas about God and man's place in the cosmos with the historical literature of the faith. For some, that literature is limited to the Bible. For most, the Bible is augmented by tradition, various other writings and the authority of current Christian leadership. In any case, the Bible is consistently held in high esteem.

Its translation from the original Hebrew, Greek and Aramaic texts can create divisions of practice as well as can its interpretation. So called "Fundamentalists" tend to translate and interpret the Bible literally unless the passage under review is clearly symbolic, metaphorical or poetic in nature. Prophetic passages are uniquely troublesome as they often include several types of literary construction. It would be fair to say, however, that most Americans, who adhere to the basic theology of Christianity, view the Bible mystically giving it reverence without needing or even wanting a comprehensive knowledge of its contents.

The overwhelming majority of Christianity's adherents in America (this includes those who are only nominally "Christian") do not read the Bible on a regular basis. Most struggle to recite familiar passages correctly and therefore depend heavily on the clergy to provide reliable instruction. It is this dependence that fosters Christianity's breakdown into denominations and sects. It is also the reason Christianity is so widely criticized among non-adherents and the community of intellectuals for its lack of coherence and consistency.

There existed a greater unanimity of theological agreement among American Christians in the first 150 years of the nation's history. In those years the Bible was a singular treasure in the Christian home. It was used in public schools, frequently read and even familiar to non-adhering citizens. In succeeding decades, the introduction of radio, television and even newer forms of electronic media increasingly displaced Bible reading. Christians grew largely ignorant of its contents and therefore more nominally "Christian." A "nominal" Christian is simply a person who identifies themselves with the name without having to accept or even know what that name implies theologically.

Today, in varying degrees, American Christians build their personal belief structures around information provided for them within their own local church or through the steady stream of teaching available to them over Christian television and radio networks. Whereas in past generations Christian theology was consistent over large social groups the last 60 years has seen the common dogma degenerate into a much more personal and individualistic belief structure very much like those individuals who place their faith in themselves. As biblical literacy has declined the theology has suffered mutations that make generalizations difficult to support if one were to look for that support in the behavior of individuals who simply claim to be Christian.

Is there a remnant of theological consistency that might help the self-faith individual or anyone else understand those who today place their faith in the God of Christianity? The following theological statements would qualify as concepts widely accepted among self-proclaimed American Christians who still hold to its traditional theology:

1. God is. As creatures, humans are incapable of either fully understanding or describing the fullness of God's character. God must therefore describe himself through self-

revelation which He has done through Scripture and intervention into Human history in the lives of his prophets and, in particular, the person of Jesus Christ.

2. God's self-revelation is progressive. Given man's limitations God has revealed his character in stages of history, first to individual men and women, next to the Hebrews as a nation (Israel), and finally, to all of mankind through the incarnation of Jesus.

3. God is holy. Through the progressive revelation of his own character God has established the necessity of righteousness evidenced by complete and unwavering obedience to his commands. Anything less is sin which separates mankind from God. The separation is complete and redemption is only available through a blood sacrifice. That form of sacrifice was first demonstrated to individuals with whom God spoke and then to the Hebrew nation – the rules for which are contained in God's law given to Moses at Mount Sinai and, finally completed once and for all through the death and resurrection of Jesus.

4. Mankind is sinful. In varying degrees, American Christians understand and accept what is commonly called the "fallen nature" of mankind. Some Christians believe humans are born free of sin but eventually sin of their own volition. Others believe that humans are actually born into sin and that Christ's

atonement is required even for those new born children who do not have the intellectual or spiritual capacity to accept or reject Christ. In those cases, the atonement is appropriated to the newborn through the mediation of the Church or the parents.

5. Humans are spiritual beings and their spirits do not die with their material bodies but proceed into an eternal existence where Jesus will judge them worthy of heaven or hell. This belief is also coupled with the understanding that all of humanity will eventually be resurrected from the dead (just as Christ arose from his grave) in bodily (material) form.

These five theological beliefs are certainly not an exhaustive list of Christianity's tenets but serve the purpose of broadly describing the fundamental points of agreement among those Americans who claim to be Christians and still hold to traditional Christian theology. These views significantly differ from those held by self-faith Americans and, when placed in the context of daily social behavior, serve to explain critical differences in economic and political policies they support.

One or two examples can be considered. In terms of life on this planet American Christians are prone to think of the cosmos as God's creation but not his full dominion. God's dominion reaches even beyond the cosmos into dimensions unknown to any creature – humanity included. As such, they are less likely to think that humanity can affect the long term existence of earth or any other planet. While

Christians see the necessity of good resource management (the biblical God instructed mankind to take *dominion* over the earth) they are not, on the whole, hand-wringing worry warts over the long term impact of greenhouse gases.

Some American Christians, though certainly not all, consider that God, with infinite wisdom and knowledge created the cosmos with a plan in place for the entire history of that creation. When considering the character of the God in whom Christianity places its faith, that God created time itself as we know and understand it. Therefore, the time of the earth and all its resources to sustain humanity was preordained and known to God who exists outside of, and therefore independent of time. If so, there is little reason to doubt the abundance of resources required to sustain all of human history.

Generally, American Christians have an abiding faith that God actually supplies all of humanity's needs. No doubt this alone provides fuel for the fires of disagreement between Christians and the more self-reliant self-faith individuals who do not acknowledge a God.

Here's just one example of how that idea plays out in practice. During the 1940's and 50's the typical American public school's history teacher taught the concept of "Manifest Destiny." The concept describes the cultural reality that the nation of the 19th Century possessed an aggregate belief that God himself had ordained the greatness – even the dominion – of the United States. The God so described was not an ethereal concept but the God of Christianity.

By the 1970's, in the heat of the Viet Nam war, the concept was certainly covered in a typical classroom but with a derisive tone implying that the idea itself illustrated the conceit of America. Conceit or not, the attitude of America at the time of its expansion across the continent was firmly ensconced in and supported by a broad national faith in the God of Abraham, Isaac, Jacob and...Jesus Christ.

For American Christians, nominal or exuberant in their faith, the departure of the nation from these once broadly-held beliefs signaled a marked change in the culture. Those cultural changes, evidenced by a departure from moral absolutism (a black and white unchanging standard for morality) into a more individualistic and subjective view of morality, brought a sense of fear.

While some would suggest it mere superstition, a minority of American Christians (particularly the "religious right") see their greatest spiritual adversity emerging from within the country rather than from without. Given their belief in God's superintendence of earth and its history (and particularly the history of the United States), they fear the loss of God's blessing over the nation if it continues to depart from the objective morality contained in the Bible. The responses of Jerry Falwell and Pat Robertson immediately following the 9/11 attacks are poignant illustrations of this belief structure.

But what are the significant differences in economic or political thought between those who place their faith in God and those who choose instead to have their faith rest in themselves? For those who place their faith in the God of Christianity, the economic structure of a "perfect" society has been hotly debated. Two prominent, nearly opposite, models compete for acceptance.

The first is based generally on the history of Israel's escape from Egypt under the leadership of Moses and specifically on the witness of the first century church as recorded in Acts chapter 2, verses 42 through 45. This model suggests that a perfect economic society should be communal. The Hebrew nation, during its sojourn to the Promised Land, was fed manna (a bread-like substance that fell from heaven) daily according to their needs. They weren't allowed to accumulate more than a day's provision except on the day before the Sabbath. Believers in the earliest Christian church in Jerusalem shared all things in common. Members sold personal possessions and brought the proceeds into a storehouse for distribution to everyone according to their "needs."

The second model, also supported by various texts of Scripture suggests a vastly different reality. That model would be primarily capitalistic with a few (some would say very few) restrictions aimed at caring for the poor and otherwise dispossessed. In the world today, these two models constantly compete for prominence among nations and groups of nations. One can easily find American Christians lining up to support either of these or even modifications somewhere in the middle of the two.

Without further review one might stop here and suggest that, with respect to economic structure, those who put their faith in God and those who do not are the same. Is there a compelling theological rationale to support some form of communal sharing (communism or socialism) versus economic independence (capitalism)?

There is a difference, albeit nuanced, in the interpretation of the biblical passages used to support each economic model. Looking very carefully at the communal model and its use in both the historical Hebrew nation and the early church, one must observe that in both cases, the societies were homogenous in terms of their shared faith. Furthermore, in both cases the adherents essentially pledged their allegiance to a direct theocracy.

It is much easier to share one's abundance with others of like faith and values. When asked to make contributions to a church fund that provides relief to those who are temporarily unemployed or perhaps disabled, consent will not be difficult to find. If, on the other hand, contributions to support a cause outside the community is sought there may be more scrutiny, perhaps even an objection. When American Christians (particularly those who hold more fundamental views) are asked to pay taxes that ultimately support abortion services there have and will always be protests.

The Scriptural model of capitalism, on the other hand, is addressed in the context of a society of mixed faiths where there is no homogeneity of values. Why is that? The literature of Christianity, when taken as a whole, suggests that mankind is sinful – some would say fallen or inherently flawed. The flaw is a bent toward selfishness. In spite of the common perception in America that Christians are self-righteous prigs the faith itself holds the view that all of mankind, Christians and non-Christians alike, fall into this category. All are sinful or, put another way, selfish. In this respect, the self-faith individual and the Christian are alike and both should flourish in an economic structure like capitalism. If both types of people were asked to explain why, in theological terms, they support capitalism the answers might be different but the result is the same.

At this point in the discussion it would be good to include a more complete description of what is meant by capitalism – and especially the term "capital." It's important to clearly define this term because any discussion where the term "capital" is left open for individual interpretation will lead to confusion. "Capital" as used here is meant to include currency, human intellect and creativity, the time a human being uses to produce a product or a service and the entirety of resources required for that production. Capitalism, as an economic structure, is the system where individuals are allowed to freely accumulate all the forms of capital required to sustain themselves and accumulate further resources to sustain the individual's posterity (whether that is their offspring or their ideas).

Self-faith individuals tend to support capitalism for obvious reasons. It is personally preferable if one is looking out for themselves and wants to accumulate capital and wealth. Those self-faith individuals who, for reasons of their own, choose a socialistic view do so primarily because their view of mankind is much kinder and gentler as it relates to the fundamental nature of humanity. They are prone to believe that mankind is inherently good, not sinful, and that a socialistic or even a communistic economic model captures the good in all of mankind harnessing it for the benefit of all, including them.

What is different in the answer for those individuals who place their faith in the God of Christianity? Their theology forces them to consider the flawed nature of mankind as a whole and opt for the economic system that best captures the strengths of mankind while mollifying the harmful effects of man's selfish nature. Capitalism harnesses and directs greed. Greed is a fundamental piece of evidence in evaluating mankind's character and is, historically speaking, indisputably universal. If nothing else, the communist experiment of the Soviet Union and its failure to promote a sustainable economy for all people (as was its promise) points directly to greed among the ruling elite. What's more, those impoverished peasants throughout the hinterlands of Russia had little or no incentive to produce up to their capacity. Without the promise of retaining the product of their labor motivation evaporated. One need only return to Maslow's Hierarchy of Needs chart to see why.

Capital formation, the accumulation of economic power, is the carrot for which mankind will generally bear the stick. Capitalism is an engine, a tool, of society that fosters the exchange of value for successful goods and services. To be a successful good or service it must be attractive, useful and highly desirable. Capitalism drives otherwise selfish individuals to produce something other individuals want in order to obtain and retain the value they seek.

The real power of capitalism rests in its capital formation characteristics. As an individual moves up and through the stages of Maslow's Hierarchy of Needs, expendable capital has to be accumulated to purchase the goods sought or perhaps the time to enjoy them. Sometimes, quite often really, a lot of capital is required to invest in the productive capacity to generate a supply for future needs including the needs of future generations.

Christian theology presupposes that mankind will always personally act in self interest. However, the literature of Christian theology, especially the Bible, also mandates the believer to pay close attention to any form of societal suffering. Benevolence is part of the Christian's worship of the God in whom he places trust. It is not a behavioral quid pro quo where God withholds his blessings or makes his grace conditioned on proper behavior.

One portion of Scripture sums it up well. "Freely you have received, freely give." It may seem like parsing of words but notice that the Scripture places receiving in front of giving, not the other way around. Benevolence is part of a Christian's joy and a form of worshipping the One from whom all blessings flow.

If Christian theology so strongly supports benevolence why is it that so many "Christians" fight against various forms of Government intervention on behalf of those who suffer? Christian theology suggests that gifts should never be compulsory. Furthermore, the benevolence of the individual should be administered through the church so that the recipient clearly sees the hand of God rather than that of the Government in the gift. To reinforce that the gift received comes from a gracious God, the giver is strongly exhorted to make all benevolent gifts anonymously. "When you give, do not let your right hand know what your left hand is doing." In other words, the giving is an act of worship between the individual and God alone.

Many wonder whether Christians can or should participate in a Government (accept the duties of citizenship) in a society that does not support their view of mankind. Should Christians, for the sake of benevolence, simply accept an ever-expanding government that seeks to tax wealth in order to dispense benefits fairly among the populace?

Clearly that question is loaded with troublesome thorns. In the broadened society that is America and considering that so very many Americans are only nominal Christians and essentially ignorant of their own theology, it is very reasonable to assume that many, many people who espouse Christianity will gladly pay more in taxes if the perceived benefit to the nation as a whole motivates them toward acceptance. It is a fact that many of America's Christians hold a certain expectation that Government should be the vehicle through which national needs are met. Former President Jimmy Carter is one shining example.

However nice and amiable those particular believers are, their assent to using the Government to collect and disperse wealth is not supported by the theology of their espoused faith. It's really that simple.

Christian theology includes the familiar passage, often quoted in church and legislatures, that Christians should "render unto Caesar what is Caesar's." The quote, from Jesus himself, came when a Pharisee (essentially a lawyer within the Hebrew justice system) attempted to trick Jesus into making a treasonous statement.

He asked Jesus whether it was appropriate to pay taxes to Rome. Israel at the time was occupied by Romans who suppressed Jewish worship and oppressed Jews in general. Depending on his answer, Jesus could have made a treasonous statement against Rome by saying "no" or indicated an affinity with Rome (something his followers would not like) if he said "yes."

Jesus asked for a coin. When he received one he asked the Pharisee, "Whose face is on this coin?" The Pharisee acknowledged that the face was Caesars. It was then that Jesus essentially said, "give the government what they require in the currency they treasure." The implication, however, was that his followers should give their spiritual allegiance and what they treasured to something or someone spiritual – that would be to others in the name of God.

Regardless of what an American Christian believes theologically about the role of Government and taxation, Jesus was clear that taxes, when levied, should be paid. Fortunately the American system of Government provides a means for changing laws and/or the representatives who make or enforce those laws. No doubt a certain vocal minority of Christians, however, will always fight heavy taxation tooth and nail to the bitter end and will be doing so based on the theological underpinnings of their firmly held faith.

To summarize, history has shown that humans will consciously or subconsciously develop a theology that expresses in whom or in what their faith will be placed. That theology will predispose the individual to favor one form of economic structure over another.

At a point where essential individual needs are met, humanity will foster community through economic exchange. Theology will generally dictate economic strategy but both will precede political views or religious practices.

In the journey that is American life as we know it a great division separates Americans. Theological and economic ignorance has forced the discussion into emotional tides where virtually everyone is raising their voice rather than reinforcing their arguments. Civility is crumbling as compromise appears more and more unlikely. The question is will Americans take a journey toward unity if unity requires first a return to theological and economic literacy? Agreement on policy may not happen; it cannot happen at all without a productive dialogue.

PART TWO

## THE JOURNEY INTO POLITICS AND RELIGION

An individual's political alignment heavily depends on the theological and economic views adopted or developed even when those views are not formally taught or even fully understood. There was a time in the nation's history when that connection was much more vital. Although it is not politically correct today to attribute the emergence of America to religious pressures in England it was and remains a fact.

To this day England has a national church but it is no longer funded through public taxation. The Church of England is represented in the United States today by the Anglican and Episcopal denominations. There was not a significant difference in theology between those who left the Old World and those who remained but there were differences in practice. It's hard for Americans today to understand but throughout history things as insignificant as the method of baptism carved deep divisions and separation between Christian adherents.

In America's own history Baptists, for example, divided during the Civil War over the issue of slavery when those favoring that institution formed the Southern Baptist Convention. The Anglican and Episcopal churches in America currently face a potential rift in their mutual communion over the issue of ordaining homosexual priests. Practicing any faith (being "religious") has proved to be the most divisive aspect among humans regardless of the country or century. Denominations of Christianity have emerged from behavioral preferences as often as theological differences.

These are just a few examples illustrating that a common theology does not guarantee a common practice. In the same way, political objectives, while certainly tied to theology, have a strange way of mutating when put to the test of political practice.

The idea that political objectives are tied to one's theology is hard for most Americans to swallow. Part of the reason is that Americans generally do not distinguish any difference between the words, "theology" and "religion." In addition, the Constitutional principle of the separation of Church and State is so misunderstood that Americans typically think politics and religion should have no influence on each other at all.

The Constitutional principle does not mean that the two mutually exclude one another as was done in the Soviet Union where the Communist regime sought to replace religious affection with love and devotion to the State. Instead the principle was established in response to colonists' experiences while citizens of England. There, as in the original British colonies, taxes were collected and a portion went automatically to The Church of England for its support. This was in exclusion of all other Protestant denominations but especially the Catholic Church in Rome.

Our nation's founders sought to remove the financial link of support from the Government to a particular denomination. While there was broad theological agreement between Americans (evidenced by commonly understood biblical references, etc,) there remained significant differences in practice. For example, some denominations favored a leadership structure where pastors were assigned rather than elected by the congregation. The theological influence of faith on the Government, however, was not feared as it is today.

If Americans of this 21st Century fear anything about religion it is a State controlled by a religiously zealous subset of some religious denomination. That fear is routinely seized upon for political currency by those in the media or the Government who want to marginalize a candidate or a well organized group who support a political solution in keeping with a theological principle.

The best example, of course, is the issue of abortion. Christian theology supports the sanctity of human life. That theological principle is one of the rare examples where the denominational practice is fairly consistent across the full spectrum of adherents from Catholics to Protestants. Still, those who support the preservation of the fetus are routinely portrayed as wild-eyed radicals who support domestic terrorism (bombing clinics) or murder (killing abortion practitioners). Similarly, pro-life activists are often called baby-killers even if their political position is supported by a theological faith in the sovereignty of the individual – in this case allowing the sovereign choice of a woman.

The Constitutional principle called the separation of Church and State is contained in the First Amendment to the Constitution. The relevant portion reads, "Congress shall make no law respecting the *establishment* of religion, or prohibiting the *free exercise* thereof;" (italics mine). This portion contains two clauses, the "establishment clause" and the "free exercise clause" and that is why those terms have been italicized.

The establishment clause restricts the Government from actively setting up through word, deed or financial support a singular religion or religious practice. The Framers of the document had little to fear from other "theologies" like Islam, Buddhism, Hinduism or any number of the world's religions. They certainly did not fear Christianity in the sense that its theology presented no economic or political threat. They did not, however, want to form a Government that would forever establish one particular religious practice or denomination of Christianity or even a certain behavioral practice of the Christian theology – like the baptism, as law. That seems clear enough. The clause keeps the Government out of the Church but does not, in any way, seek to remove the influence of religion, theology or even a particular denomination of a theology from political involvement or influence.

The free exercise clause clarified that intention by making a covenant with all Americans to do nothing to prohibit them from practicing their religion regardless of its theological foundation. Thanks to the First Amendment, which also guarantees free speech, Americans have the right to express their theological faith and practice whatever religion that faith promotes. There have been rare exceptions but those exceptions have addressed practices that threaten the safety or well-being of others. Human sacrifice, for example would clearly be a "practice" not sanctioned by the First Amendment nor tolerated by the nation's founders.

The free speech clause of the First Amendment assures Americans that they can participate in free dialogue over any number of issues. That freedom also provides the right to "peaceably assemble." The breadth of religious practice in general and the abundance of Christian denominations specifically bear evidence to the success of this right. Political organizations with diametrically opposing agendas also thrive and their views can be heard through a free press that is also guaranteed by the First Amendment.

This important right guarantees a forum for argument in America. But the vehemence of verbal conflict and the anger witnessed each day can only be attributed to the fact that it is a firmly held *theology* upon which nearly every religious or political opinion rests. It is one reason people are cautioned against discussing religion or politics in mixed company.

This right has also fostered a uniquely American reality that if you have four people in a room you will have five opinions. The freedom to think and express thoughts ultimately develops opinion. Newspapers, television and radio news programs and the internet try, sometimes in vain, to separate news from opinion. Newspapers separate them by establishing an editorial and opinion section in the paper. Television and radio reserve time in a news broadcast for "commentary." The internet is much more freewheeling with mixtures of fact and fiction posing as either news or opinion.

The result is that Americans, by and large, gather themselves into social groups with shared opinions and rarely venture out to seriously discuss or consider alternate views. Within the comfortable confines of these groups (churches, labor unions, corporate boardrooms) opinions become less tested and, eventually, minds become dulled through the lack of intellectual exercise. When confronted by a differing viewpoint, many will throw up their arms in despair and say, "Well, that's *your* opinion!"

Is it possible that the anger, even violence, could be avoided altogether if proponents of opposing religious or political opinions admitted that the real issue is one of theology? A theology is basic and fundamental because, at the end of the day, all theologies are based on faith rather than reason. This is not to suggest that there is no value in rational thought but that all rational thought comes finally to rest upon an assumption and that assumption must be taken by faith.

Consider the following dialogue between two people who couldn't possibly be more at odds as they consider and share their *opinions* on the issue of polygamy:

■■■■■■■■■■■■■■■■■■■■■■■■■■■■■■■■■■■■■■■■■■■■■■■■■■■■

Jerry, a fundamentalist Mormon and a member of the Fundamentalist Church of Jesus Christ of the Latter Day Saints, sat in a diner in Santa Fe, New Mexico. His practice of polygamy was unknown to his business associates and the community at large. He lived a very discrete life in a suburban community where his four wives lived in two homes that backed up to one another. Jerry fathered seven children, split his time between the two homes but only parked in the driveway of one. On one street, Jerry was known to be living with his wife of 13 years and his wife's "sister." On the street behind Jerry's main home, lived two "sisters" who rarely socialized with anyone but the family living behind them.

As Jerry sat, drinking orange juice and reading the paper, another man, Robert, walked into the diner. Robert worked with Jerry at a local manufacturing company where Jerry was the Vice President of Sales and Robert was the company's CFO. Robert, 45 years old and about 10 years senior to Jerry, is an elder in the city's largest Methodist church. They have been good friends for a long time although they have rarely discussed anything outside of their business interests.

Robert saw Jerry sitting alone. Jerry heard a bell ring as Robert walked through the door, looked up, and smiled broadly at him. He waved Robert over to have a seat with him.  As Robert took a seat, Jerry said, "Hey Robert, it's good to see you. Sit down, join me. What brings you here on a Saturday morning?"

Robert, rubbed the back of his neck, frowned and said, "I just had to get out of the house...Janice is Spring cleaning and banished me to clean the gutters."

"Oh, that sounds bad, buddy." Jerry sympathized.

The two men went on commiserating with one another and enjoying each other's company. At some point Robert picked up the newspaper that Jerry had set to one side and put on his reading glasses to more clearly see an article just below the fold of the front page. The article's headline read, "Sheriff Responds to Curious Domestic Dispute."  Jerry noticed the furrows of concern crisscrossing Robert's forehead and uncomfortably cleared his throat.

As Robert read through the first two paragraphs he realized that the "domestic dispute" involved two teenage boys, apparently half-brothers, fist fighting in the front yard of a home where both of their mothers lived together. A man, alleged to be both boys' father, was badly beaten by the older of the two boys when he attempted to break up the fight. The report said the family was part of a polygamist community. Robert set the paper down, took his glasses off and said, "I don't see how anyone can justify polygamy. There are laws against it. I wonder when this State is going to crack down on these people, it just isn't right!"

Jerry shifted in his seat, considering whether or not it was worth defending his own deeply held belief in polygamy. He thought about the stress he endured each and every day simply trying to practice a religious rite that he felt was completely consistent with his faith. He rarely tried to convince anyone outside his religion but was tired of the isolation he felt. He decided to venture into a discussion. "Robert, why should anyone have to justify or condemn polygamy?"

Robert absently turned a page in the paper and said, "Well, no one has to condemn it, that's already been done by the law. I *would* like to see someone try to justify it, though." He looked at Jerry and saw his conflicted expression. "Jerry," he asked, "you sympathetic to these people?"

Jerry turned his eyes downward, staring at and beyond his juice. Looking up with resolve he said, "Robert, I'm not sympathetic to *those* people." He paused and drained the glass, "I am one of those people!"

Robert set the paper down laughing at what he thought was Jerry being funny. When Jerry's expression indicated otherwise he swallowed hard. His mind raced through four or five responses as an uncomfortable moment passed. Finally he spoke, "You're telling me that you are a polygamist? I don't believe it."

"Believe it. I have four wives, Robert, and I'm sick of living as if there is something wrong with that. All are happy and committed to the principle. I live a quiet and productive life; what business does the State have telling me who can be a part of my family?"

Shocked, Robert sat back in his seat and shifted. He considered Jerry's question. "The State can't stop you from believing whatever you want, Jerry, but the State does have an interest in protecting the rights of women and children. The principle, as you call it, is nothing but a way to justify men taking advantage of and dominating women. Look at the results! How could a young man, growing up under that kind of arrangement ever respect women when they see nothing but subservient behavior in their mothers?

"What about young girls? Are you telling me that a girl should grow up trained to share a man? The principle, as you call it, is also completely impractical. Just where will the young men in your system go to find wives when a few men in the movement marry all the women in the community? Isn't that why so many young men are banished and left to fend for themselves in the streets of Santa Fe?"

Jerry placed his hands palms down on the table. He hoped his body language would keep the discussion calm. "First of all, Robert, you're making some pretty big assumptions. What makes you automatically think that women in our community aren't respected? My relationship with each one of my wives is no different than the one you have with yours. You got pushed out of the house to clean the gutters this morning by who," he paused, "by your wife. My wives stand up for themselves all the time! For you to imagine that I don't respect them is insulting. I not only respect them, Robert, I love them and my children know it.

"My children, by the way, love and respect them as well. They obey all of the mothers equally. As far as my daughters are concerned, they will have to make a choice of who to marry one day just like all my wives did. I'm not holding a gun to their head and they all have two legs. They can walk away from our faith anytime they want. Those boys that you say are banished? They just walked away, Robert. We don't have a secret police pushing them out to the streets of this city. My sons are all under ten years old right now. They know we're different but they also know how much I love them and want them to be a part of our family in heaven."

Robert's posture eased backwards and his face lines smoothed as he tried to relax. "Jerry, I'm sorry if I offended you. I'm trying real hard to take this information in. It's quite a shock, really. Look, I know that you're a good guy. We've worked together for a long time and I respect your professional skills. I don't want this to come between us. At the same time, I wonder if we could discuss this calmly as friends." He smiled and added, "I doubt you'll change my mind or that I'll change yours but I would love to discuss this with you because, frankly, I enjoy the intellectual exercise. I just want to be careful not to offend or take offense if we talk about this."

Jerry smiled and let out a long breath. "To tell you the truth, Robert, I have never told anyone in the world outside my religion about my life. I'd like to think that I can trust you to keep this discussion between us. There's really no reason for this information to get out at the office. Do you know what I mean?"

"Sure." Robert affirmed. "But, Jerry, if you're truly not ashamed of your beliefs why keep them a secret? I mean I would never share this information with anyone without your permission but if you're convinced that you have every right to practice something that is against the law why not put your case to the authorities and accept the results?"

Jerry smiled, "If you were to read in tomorrow's paper that the State enacted a law making masturbation illegal, how many Methodists would line up in front of the courthouse to protest?"

Robert smiled and lightly chuckled, "I see your point." He already knew that Jerry had a good sense of humor. "Look, uh Jerry," he began with caution; "I'd like to understand your point of view. To be honest, I've never taken the opportunity to just talk calmly to someone from your church. I mean, sure, I had some young men from the LDS knock on my door but they weren't there to listen, know what I mean?"

Jerry leaned forward and lowered his voice; "If we're going to talk about this, I'm going to suggest that we do something I tell my salespeople to do all the time."

"What's that?"

"I tell them that all people want to buy things; the best salespeople in the world know how and when to get out of their way. Robert, the reason these kinds of discussions turn ugly is that human beings tend to be so focused on making their own points that they forget to listen, truly listen, to the other person. If we're going to talk about this, I'd like to know that we're each spending as much energy listening as talking."

Robert smiled, "That's really good, Jerry. Do you mind if I use that? I have some analysts working in payroll who need to hear that piece of advice." He raised an empty coffee cup toward his server and smiled his requests for more liquid brain food. "I know you don't drink coffee, Jerry, but I think I'll 'listen' better if I have another cup."

"If you'll promise to listen, Robert, I'll buy the coffee." Jerry laughed.

■■■■■■■■■■■■■■■■■■■■■■■■■■■■■■■■■■■■■■■■■■■■■■■■■■■

It's a good time to interrupt this story. The telling has so far been a bit idyllic. Wouldn't it be wonderful if people did what these two guys are about to do – agree to chat about a fundamental disagreement in an agreeable way? Where do you suppose the conversation will go? How will Robert and Jerry choose to make their points? Is it really likely that they will expend as much energy listening as talking? While reading the story did you find yourself identifying with one or the other of the men? Did you form opinions or think about what you would have liked to have said in their place?

Wouldn't it be interesting if everyone reading this stopped here, at this point, and wrote the rest of the dialogue? Sketching out a discussion between two adversaries is one of the principle tools philosophers have used over the centuries to make their points. It's a powerful way to control the direction of an argument and is called "dialectic."

The point of using it here is not to convince the reader of any particular point of view but to convince the reader that, at the end of the day, dialectics are full of unproven presuppositions that ultimately rest on one final assumption. That assumption will be something taken by faith.

Eventually, Robert and Jerry will come down to a final proposition to consider. Robert will have demonstrated that his life and values are based on a traditional view of the God of the Bible and the moral imperatives driven by that faith. Jerry, on the other hand, will agree with those imperatives to the point where he moves beyond the Bible and places his faith on the God and theology Joseph Smith redefined in the Book of Mormon. If they do manage to have a peaceful dialogue, then they will likely part as friends who base their lives on different theologies. Each will have opinions that cannot be compromised without feeling as though they're abandoning their faith. Abandoning one's faith is a very serious thing to demand and yet Americans on the left and right of the political spectrum are asked to do that on a daily basis.

This is a great place, just as a reminder, to repeat the paragraph that preceded Jerry and Robert's story:

"Is it possible that the anger, even violence, could be avoided altogether if proponents of opposing religious or political opinions admitted that the real issue is one of theology? A theology is basic and fundamental because, at the end of the day, all theologies are based on faith rather than reason. This is not to suggest that there is no value in rational thought but that all rational thought comes finally to rest upon an assumption and that assumption must be taken by faith."

Since theology is something Americans rarely discuss in public and since our Congressional leaders and Presidents dutifully try to avoid it, the people of this Country tend to think along narrowly defined political lines. People are generally grouped along political party lines or, more recently, described as liberal, conservative, or moderate. Unfortunately these words are wholly inadequate theologically. It's not that people in these groups don't have consistencies in their theology but that the foundational faith behind each view is either ignored or just not understood. Through lack of use, we are a theologically illiterate people.

It would be easy to argue here that Americans are not just theologically illiterate. While the country enjoys a relatively high level of literacy – the ability to read and write – our educational system is producing graduates who have no interest in or ability to produce cogent political or religious thought. Over the past four decades the arguments between the political left and right have become increasingly strident and emotional. At the same time, Americans have a growing frustration over the reality that having one party or the other in power makes little or no difference in the resulting direction of the Country.

Without a clear and reasonably linear thought pattern supporting political ideas back to their theological foundation, the Country drifts along on the momentum of the only other thing Americans mostly share in common: Economic self interest. Whether one places faith in "that beyond which nothing greater can be conceived" or in their own sovereignty, the impact on economic thinking will be largely the same. Self-faith individuals, looking out for number one, will not generally submit to a "share-the-wealth" plan and those who believe in the Christian God will do the same given their acknowledgement that mankind's greed (the flaw) must be harnessed for good and is largely harnessed by capitalism.

It would not be intellectually honest to leave the preceding paragraph without acknowledging that there are millions of Americans who do believe in sharing the wealth. They do so out of a deeply held theological belief that mankind is inherently good (without flaw) and that, together, humans can coalesce around that economic ideal and build a world of peace and harmony based on giving people what they need out of the abundance of what all humanity has. It just hasn't been proved in social history but frequently does exist in one place, the individual family. But, even in that basic social unit self-interest often explodes into conflicts over who gets the car on Saturday night.

If it is true that all economic, political and religious thought finds its root in theology, what was the theological foundation of America?

Much has already been written about the intentions of the founding fathers of this nation when they created the Constitution. There is little that can be productively added. Americans today, depending on their political affiliation, essentially hold one of two views about the value of considering the framer's *intentions* when interpreting the meaning of the Constitution's articles and the Bill of Rights (the first 10 amendments).

Those who favor a flexible interpretation that considers the changing tides of political opinion and the short terms needs of the public give less heed to the intentions of the framers and are called non-originalists. They are derisively called "activists" because they create law through decisions which might otherwise be too difficult to pass through the legislature.

Those who favor the sturdiness of the Constitution and prefer legislative action to change or amend the document are called originalists. Perhaps the most famous originalist is Robert Bork who, when nominated to the Supreme Court by Republican President Ronald Reagan, was not confirmed by the Democrat-controlled Senate. His extensive writings and his answers before the Senate Judiciary committee provided ample ammunition to sink his nomination. It is now common to expect strict originalists, like Judge Bork, to be "Borked" if presented to a Senate controlled by the left. Bork's defense of originalism is summed up in his quote, "The truth is that the judge who looks outside the

Constitution always looks inside himself and nowhere else."

Over the past 50 years a few key polarizing issues have emerged in the American conversation that have severely tested the nation's confidence in the process whereby the constitutionality of laws are considered. When a law's constitutionality is tested in American courts the final arbiter is the nation's Supreme Court. There, nine justices, each having been nominated by a sitting President and confirmed by the United States' Senate to a lifelong term, consider the law's harmony with the Constitution as it has been amended. When the nation is evenly divided over a particular issue the Supreme Court's decision on that issue will inevitably be greeted with angst by nearly half of the populace.

The most divisive issues are driven by moral imperatives based upon an individual's view of right and wrong, good and evil, in short – their theology or world view. These issues have a clear theological foundation whether individuals recognize them or not. As discussed most Americans are largely ignorant of theology in general and the religious affiliations they enjoy don't necessarily inspire a significant depth of specific literacy in their expression. Without that depth of theological understanding the issues are emotionally explosive and often provoke public demonstrations. Abortion, homosexual marriage, stem-cell research, capital punishment and war are just a few examples of issues that tend to divide the country rather evenly along party and, in the end, theological lines.

As these issues prompt action within Congress, narrowly passed bills are signed into law but are ultimately tested in federal courts where the defining issues emerge and the lines of constitutional interpretation are drawn. There, justices will apply their interpretation and that interpretation will be largely motivated by mixtures of originalist methodology and/or their own theological views of what is ultimately good and evil.

The Constitution itself is an amazing piece of literature in that it expresses the fundamental basis under which individual freedoms are preserved in a democratic republic. Most of its provisions are written as negative rights expressing what the government cannot do rather declaring what it can or must do. This is the principle reason granting new rights remains difficult. Some rights may not be positively proscribed in the Constitution and therefore have to be "read into" (activism) or created (the originalists' preference) through amendments by Congress.

For example, the right to free speech (the first amendment) is something the government cannot infringe upon (negatively stated) and the right to the free exercise of religion cannot be prohibited. The framers built into the Constitution presuppositions that, for them, were "self-evident." One of those "self-evident" presuppositions was that man's role in ruling over other men was so predisposed to corruption that limitations had to be placed on the Government rather than upon the governed.

This view was codified in the Declaration of Independence with the words of the preamble:

"We hold these truths to be self-evident, that all men are created equal, that they are endowed by their Creator with certain unalienable rights, that among these are Life, Liberty and the pursuit of Happiness. That to preserve these rights, Governments are instituted among men, deriving their just powers from the consent of the governed."

This view was reinforced in the opening line of the Constitution where it began with, "We the People..."

Popular, though not necessarily accurate, opinions of the founding fathers' intentions have been offered for public consideration. Likewise, accurate, though not necessarily popular views have as well. Historical interpretations of events often follow the preference of the ultimate winner in the dispute – after the fact. For example, the southern States called their conflict with the northern States the "War Between the States" the northern victors were ultimate arbiters of what became "correct" history and the war was then called the Civil War and the South's actions an "insurrection."

The intentions of the founding fathers have been established, erased, re-established and erased again over and over according to the tides of public opinion. The task of genuine historians (though not necessarily Supreme Court justices) is to separate the emotional yearnings of present-day revisionists and attempt to capture the real essence of the people and institutions of a particular historic event like those attitudes and belief structures of the founding fathers.

Of the 56 signatories of the Declaration of Independence, all but five were Protestants, one was Catholic and four (Thomas Jefferson, Ben Franklin, John Adams, and Robert Treat Pain) were either Deists or Unitarian. Deists and Unitarians are not considered aligned with "Christian Theology." It is not insignificant that the writer of the Declaration was Thomas Jefferson – a Deist. It should be remembered, however, that he himself admitted that the document contained nothing "new" but was the result of pieces added here and there from other colonial documents and the advice of other committee members. There is little evidence that the signatories of the document suddenly converted to a Deist theology just because Jefferson wrote the Declaration.

Of the 48 signatories of the Articles of Confederation, all but two were Protestants, one was Catholic and one, Cornelius Harnett, was a Deist.

Of the 55 delegates to the Constitutional Convention in 1787, 49 were Protestants, three were Catholic and the rest were unaffiliated. It is not a historical stretch to say that the founding fathers shared a common Christian theology – at least tacitly so. Of course, it does not follow that each and every "Christian" delegate considered themselves a strict adherent to the theological precepts of Christianity. Some signatories were relatively unconcerned with religion at all. It is in the language of the documents themselves, particularly the Declaration of Independence, where one can see that a commonly shared theology heavily influenced the framers.

The framers were, in the case of the Declaration, looking for the theological means to disassociate themselves collectively from the English Monarchy. Monarchial ascension was then considered a divine right administered by the Church be that in Rome or in Canterbury. The idea that a people could democratically govern themselves without a monarch was not necessarily new but previous attempts – even in England – had failed.

Although it was the reformation that ultimately motivated colonist to seek religious freedom in America, the European centers of that reformation, Germany, Holland, Scandinavia and England were still ruled by monarchs. If the colonist were going to declare independence they had to do so in terms that not only did not conflict with Christianity but could be supported by it. The preamble of the Declaration makes an appeal to the "Laws of Nature and of Nature's God" when supporting the decision to "dissolve the political bands holding them to England while *establishing a separate and equal station to which that Law and God entitled them*." (Italics mine)

Was it their intention to establish a theocratic government? The text of the document does not support that at all. In fact, the intention to establish a Government unhampered by religion compelled them to instead create a government Abraham Lincoln described as of, for and by the people. Yet that Government would have no affinity for the people without a theologically sound foundation upon which the people could build their future hopes. The document does not remove God from the conversation but instead appeals to the blessings only God could give. The document expressly places the judgment of their actions before the "Supreme Judge of the world." That "Judge" was the only one they commonly "knew." In order to secure the support of the colonists, they would appeal to the God of their common faith – the God of Abraham, Isaac, Jacob and Jesus Christ.

But the Declaration of Independence did not, by itself, establish the United States; it merely separated the colonies from English rule. The Constitution, signed and ratified in 1787, did that and is the document upon which American law rests. Are there foundational concepts embodied in the Constitution that rely on a singular theology? If so, is that theology Christian or is it a theology based on self-faith?

Regardless of what others have written or opined about the Constitution it is an extremely neutral document. It is law. As such, it embodies very little that can be construed as either theology or religious. In plain language it outlines the methods by which the American States cede national control to a Federal Government. The States place an historic reliance on individual men. It establishes a representative form of government that never separates ultimate control from the citizenry. To safeguard that control, no power in the government is left without significant "checks and balances" to inhibit tyranny. It includes appropriate restrictions on the majority to assure all Americans that a significant minority will not be completely powerless.

There is a common theme that can only be read between its lines in the ethereal space of reason its words invoke. That theme is that sovereignty, the effectual power to act upon others, is reserved to the individual who has received that "endowment" (a word from the Declaration) from the ultimate Sovereign, the Creator, in the form of free will. Through the democratic republic, established by the Constitution, individuals use their right to vote as a means of collectively delegating their individual sovereignty to representatives who then, in congress with one another, coordinate efforts to protect and defend the nation while continuously guaranteeing the rights of the individual.

This system communicates two basic principles to anyone willing to listen and understand. First, it recognizes that ultimate Sovereignty comes from something or someone beyond which nothing greater can be conceived – God. It also accepts and codifies a principle laid out in the pages of the Bible – that man is a free moral agent endowed by God with the rights and means of self-determination. Ironically, that endowment allows all of humanity to individually accept or reject the God from whose hand those rights and means emanate. While it is clear that the founders of America held that truth to be self evident, they nonetheless granted as fact that fellow citizens of the new nation would never be compelled to accept that premise or any theology in particular. Instead, they placed their confidence in the power of delegated sovereignty which would ensure that raw power could neither be concentrated enough to thwart the will of the people as a whole nor void the ultimate will of the Sovereign Creator, whether that Creator was believed to exist or not.

The conclusion is rather obvious, isn't it? America's form of government and its historic economic structure is based on a theology but the government's form does not force that theology onto the governed. The result is that Americans at large are free to place their faith in either themselves as Sovereign or in that beyond which nothing greater can be conceived.

Theology forms the basis upon which individuals, who choose to live in society with one another, form their economic and political structure along with religious practice. It is possible, even historically probable, that the economic structure of a society will emerge first and determine its ultimate longevity.

While it is possible for individuals with differing theologies to agree on a singular form of economic structure (capitalism, communism or something in between) it is improbable that a fundamental economic structure will endure within a fractured political and religious environment unless that economic structure is widely believed to embody truth in a theological sense.

Those who practice economics professionally will sometimes admit that economics is an art rather than a science. There is scientific research that goes into describing economic behavior and there are behavioral sciences that attempt, at least, to explain human behavior. Economic indicators find their expression in mathematics –surely that is a science! But economics, like the weather, is subject to what some call the "butterfly effect." The butterfly effect is tied to chaos theory and, as the description implies, illustrates how even the tiniest of changes in the system can gather all the forces of chaos and change the direction of the weather or, in this case, the economy.

Honest economists will eventually admit that their predictions of economic behavior are merely theoretical. Theoretically, a tax cut should promote spending as individuals enjoy an increase in their disposable income. That increase should (and frequently does) result in consumer spending that then fuels economic growth. Theoretically, deficit spending (a government spending more cash than it has on hand) puts that government into a position of borrowing money in competition for the pool of money available for all private and public spending. The result is less predictable because on the one hand, the government's spending, just like individual spending, fuels economic growth but that growth can be partly or wholly offset by the increased cost of debt to the private sector of the economy.

If you're experiencing a dull throbbing pain between your eyes, you're certainly not alone. The arguments supporting or opposing various economic policies happen in the realm of political practice. They are lived, however, around American's kitchen tables where getting louder often wins the day. The arguments take on additional emotional momentum when individuals within the family are under economic stress. Nothing motivates Americans more stridently than the vagaries of the economy where government policies that are intended to help large segments of the populace hit some Americans where it hurts – in their wallets.

At America's founding, the economic structure of unimpaired capitalism was widely accepted. Economic theories competing with capitalism would not really emerge until more revolutions in Europe and the rise of individualism gave philosophers motivation to explore alternate ideas. Communism, for example, would not enjoy broad discussion for another century.

While America continued its expansive and accelerated growth the economic discussion was somewhat limited to monetary policy (that's how to establish a currency and protect its value). Fiscal policy (how the government spends money) was hampered by the fact that the federal government's bank account was strictly limited to those fund-raising means approved by the individual States. There was no federal income tax until the Sixteenth Amendment to the Constitution was ratified in 1913.

Throughout the history of this nation there have always been fringe elements of extraordinarily small number that sought a change in the fundamental structure of the government. By and large, however, Americans continue to retain faith in the structure of its democratic republic. That consensus, however, has been more and more severely tested as political parties waver between the capitalistic economic structure the nation originally adopted and competing economic models introduced on the European continent since 1913. The advent of the income tax not only enlarged this nation's government as a competing entity with the private sector but deficit spending by government has systematically eroded the effect capitalism has on economic growth.

Still, it is nonsense to claim that unlimited capitalism does not produce inequities in society. Just as history has proven the inadequacies of communism it has proven that, without some regulation, capitalism will produce a large middle class surrounded by extraordinary wealth on one hand and extraordinary poverty on the other. These extremes finally moved government to enact laws that regulated powerful industries and protected individuals who could not otherwise compete for capital. Remember individuals need capital every bit as much as companies. Without a reasonably inexpensive way to accumulate capital, individuals will not be able to thrive. If capital is restricted so much as to be concentrated only among the wealthy or anonymous corporations individuals may struggle to survive – let alone thrive.

Whether fully understood or not the nation's government has generally opted to limit capitalism's powerfully productive engine through small adjustments. These have been put into place through either tax policy or regulation of big industries. Some will say that the New Deal (Franklin Roosevelt's plan for coming out of the Great Depression) brought *massive* changes rather than just *small adjustments*. That is certainly correct in terms of the times the legislation was passed. But the nation's history since then has demonstrated that the trend which began with the New Deal has, in the last three decades, become a movement supported by those who would prefer to restructure the economy entirely. Some Americans would like to move away from capitalism and into something that would be best defined as socialism.

Throughout these changes in economic policy the two major political parties have divided along the lines of capitalism and socialism. Since World War II, and leading up to and through the Reagan Administration, economic policies of differing nuance found support within both major parties. Those associated with the Democrat Party became identified as "liberal" and wore that label with pride as long as the description was limited to social policy. Southern democrats, for example, would sometimes add that they were "fiscally conservative" (meaning that they still supported capitalism's essential structure) and it was those fiscal conservatives who supported Ronald Reagan and his economic policies through two terms.

In the northeast and far west, traditional Republican districts elected officials that steadfastly held "fiscally conservative ideals" while being more "socially liberal." This self-labeling indicated their empathy for those constituents who increasingly expressed fears that "social (and religious) conservatives" in America aimed to eliminate their right to engage in behaviors considered outside the nation's historically mainstream religious foundation. Over the past 60 years questions of personal behaviors that do not comply with traditional Christian morality have demanded an answer.

America's social liberals, whether they are in the Democratic or Republican parties, have supported a departure from America's theological roots by seeking to elevate the sovereignty of humanity. The effect is to introduce a morality that shifts according to the individual as opposed to being fixed in the precepts of the God of the Bible. Meanwhile, the liberal economic policy of expanding government and its intervention in regulating capital growth seemed to actually provide support for the moral decay conservative Christians feared most. The liberal social agenda, which included tolerance of alternative lifestyles, was supported by economic policies that expanded government oversight into the means of guaranteeing the rights of individuals to behave in ways formerly thought incongruent with Christianity.

It was during the Reagan administration that something unique emerged in the public dialogue. Critical policy decisions, whether social or economic, were encountering support or adversity in America's religious pulpits. The emergence of a strong voting block of religious conservatives surprised the public (particularly the media) and quickly organized itself into a powerful interest group led by prominent evangelical preachers. These preachers appealed to the historical roots of America, particularly those religious roots, and built a self-described "moral majority." Whether the group was, in fact, a majority in America was not important. What was important is that the group took a strong foothold in the Republican Party and together elected a President who was sympathetic to their interpretation of history and theology.

Riding a wave of self-satisfaction the power of the religious right continued to openly express itself through media outlets it created and funded both in television and radio. To presume that this constituency's influence was limited to only members of their choir requires as much delusion as they are routinely accused of possessing by the mainstream media. Liberal thinkers in America had become used to the idea that the Constitution's separation of Church and State clause protected them from religious interference into social policy.

Meanwhile, the economic structure of communism or more moderate forms of socialism found increasing support among America's liberal thinkers and European parliaments throughout the 20th Century.

It gathered strength during the cold-war years and reached a new high during the turbulent Viet Nam era and the social revolutions of the 1960's and 70's.

During the 1980's this intellectual division in America began to get emotional. Reagan called out the liberals in government telling the American people that government wasn't the solution. "Government," he said, "was the problem." Recognizing a theological difference in the foundations of capitalism and communism, Reagan called the Soviet Union an evil empire at a time when the popularity of the movie, *Star Wars*, gave all Americans a dramatic visual representation of this rhetoric.

Yet even as the Soviet Union crumbled under its own debt and hapless productivity, liberals steadfastly held to its unproven economic principles. As a "theory" communism works perfectly. Even if considered a "science" it only appears to work in the isolation of the laboratory. But associated with the practice of communism in Russia was the harsh policy that replaced religious faith with Communism's own theology... worship of the State.

It was this theological affront along with the liberal's deep empathy for an economic system that advanced their agenda to which religious conservatives in both parties responded when they elected Reagan and, subsequently, shepherded Republican, George Herbert Walker Bush, Reagan's Vice President into his own term as President.

During Reagan's two terms in office the Moral Majority's icons of leadership became distracted by high-profile evangelical leaders caught in sensational moral failures. A rather quick succession of these failures seemed to lull the powerful block of voters into a guilty silence. George Bush, a reluctant partner in Reagan's meteoric rise was certainly faithful to the precepts of the far-right during his Vice Presidency but failed in one particular moment to fully understand the wounded conservative giant.

On October 27, 1990, he signed new legislation into law that, in an effort to balance the budget, broke his campaign promise of "no new taxes" and thereby alienated the fiscally conservative base of the Republican Party along with the masses of the religious right who, while certainly fiscally conservative, were becoming more alarmed by Bush's apparent affinity with liberal theology. His choice to override his promise to America was seen by some as moral ambiguity.

A recession late in the Bush presidency pried open the door for Bill Clinton and one campaign phrase, coined by political strategist, James Carville, blew it open. The phrase, "it's the economy, stupid," served to diminish the perception of Bush's intelligence while also focusing a laser-like beam in a direction of economic and social moderation. Since that time Republicans, both religious and non-religious, have enjoyed a somewhat reluctant fellowship built around a capitalistic economic policy, in opposition to an enlarged government-driven social agenda favored by the left, while giving lip service if not full support to a somewhat quieter "moral majority's" ethical mandates.

The years leading up to the present day have been filled with further posturing on both sides of the political spectrum. However, the intensity of the argument and the dramatic lines drawn between the left and right have never been clearer. Economic policy has become a line drawn in the sand separating those on the left who have a heightened view of man's goodness and therefore favor an active government that secures economic equality for all and those on the right who continue to believe in man's flawed nature and seek to harness greed for everyone's benefit with a combination of capitalistic motivation tempered by a return to traditional American values.

The urgent problem with this state of affairs is that the nation, having split over two economic models whose theological foundations could not be more dissimilar, must find a way toward practical and unifying compromise without nullifying essential theological faiths. The founding fathers of our nation had the tremendous advantage of working with a relatively homogeneous populace. The fracturing of America along religious, economic, and political lines puts the nation at severe risks and increasing the amplitude of today's arguments will not bring a resolution. It could, however, bring on another revolution.

In times of eminent crisis and danger, America has traditionally found or discovered leadership in the office of the President. The Constitution, however, does not give the President legislative or judicial power. The President's job is to execute the laws of the land and provide a level of control over a policy's implementation. But the real power of the Presidency today rests in the President's power to persuade.

With just a little over a year in Barak Obama's presidency his favorability index has fallen below 46% among the American people and Congress' favorability is below 20%. It's not really unusual for a President's favorability to drop as low as his/her base constituency (a hardcore group that generally registers between 30 and 35%). But when a persistent opinion of Congress (that does have legislative power) drops into the high teens Americans have reason to be frightened.

# PART THREE

## MONEY, MONEY, MONEY

Here's an interesting exercise with just a little bit of simple math. Assume that a typical United States Congressman really wants to be "in touch" with constituents. The motivation is so strong a ground-breaking decision is made to personally talk with every citizen at least once during every term. Inspired by the thought the Congressman instructs the staff to calculate how much time he could devote to the citizens of his district if he wanted to reach them all.

The staff painstakingly goes to work. They calculate there are 52 weeks in a year with roughly 5 working days each week. Knowing their boss is a particularly hard working Congressman, they assume a 10-hour work day. In two years the Congressman will work 5,200 hours or about 312,000 minutes. Wow, they think, that's a lot of work! However, the average House district in the United States represents 646,000 citizens, the smallest about 410,000. The staff, armed with this powerful information reports back to their boss that working non-stop, 10 hours a day throughout the term, he will be able to devote 29 seconds of time to each citizen.

Frustrated, the Congressman lectures his staff that there are other responsibilities he must tend to if he is to be a member of Congress. He has to vote, attend and occasionally even make speeches in committee hearings, travel back and forth to the district, write letters, appear on television news shows (at least occasionally) and he has to devote additional time to the most important constituents and their lobbyists. He reminds them that he does want to be re-elected.

Suddenly, he snaps his fingers and exclaims he has a great idea. Opening the top drawer of his ornate desk he reaches in and pulls a newspaper clipping he saved from the last election. Shuffling the paper to his top aide he instructs him to only focus on the constituents who actually voted in the last election. The aide, always supportive of the boss, exclaims that's a great idea. Why bother with those who don't vote anyway? The aide takes the clipping, looks at the election results and happily reports that only 61% of registered voters actually voted in the 2008 elections – a presidential election year. (It's generally less than 50% in an off-election year).

The Congressman is beginning to see a plan come into focus. He tells the aide to look at the results again and figure out how many votes he received in the last election. The aide smiles and tells his boss that he tallied nearly 210,000 votes, or about 53% of those who voted, and then reminds his boss again about the great job he did winning those votes. The Congressman takes a moment for self admiration in the mirror but still isn't completely satisfied because, after all, time must be used wisely. Even if he focused all of his time on just those who voted for him he could only devote about 90 seconds of personal discussion to each one.

A wiser, more experienced, aide walks into the Congressman's office and makes a declaration. Reviewing the Congressman's schedule over the past four months the wise aide informs the boss that, on average, he has but one hour a day that he can personally devote to actually speaking with constituents.

Exasperated, the Congressman decides his constituents will just have to rely on newspaper reports, his monthly newsletter, his congressional website, e-mail, letters, and his weekly telephone speeches (sent by autodial to those interested enough to give out their personal phone numbers).

Recalling the last election once more his takes comfort in the fact that he only spent $1.4 million on his last campaign and $1.1 million of that came from political action committees (lobbyist organizations) and individuals donating at least $1,000. If he wants to be re-elected he just needs to focus on those people.

If he can convince 800 constituents to donate $1,000 each and collect $300,000 from interest groups, he'll only need another $300,000 in small donations to get elected again. Surely out of the 210,000 people who voted for him in the last election he can find 10,000 who will give at least $30. He muses to himself that it really only takes 10,800 people to get him elected – that, he thinks, is doable. After all, if he really only has one hour a day to directly connect with constituents (that's 520 hours per congressional term) he'll be able to spend nearly 3 minutes with each of the 10,800 donors and, amazingly, he'll be raising about $2,700 per hour of work. That's more than he ever made as an attorney!

Hasn't this been an enlightening exercise? Consider this: the average congressional district election cost the winner $1.4 million in 2008. If the winner won with the same percentage of vote as President

Obama, (53%) and therefore received about 210,000 votes, the winner paid a mere $6.67 per vote. Think about that the next time you're asked to make a political donation to a congressional candidate. A $30 dollar donation buys four and half votes.

There's more to consider here. The margin of victory for the average candidate was about 6% or roughly 24,000 votes. To reverse the result – to spend a loser into a winner – it would require turning 12,001 of those votes in the other direction. At $6.67 per vote the margin of victory just means outspending the opponent by $80,000.

This is not, by the way, really scientific at all – there are, admittedly, other factors that go into winning an election. No amount of spending can turn a poor candidate into a good one or even keep a good one from saying the wrong thing at the wrong time. But it's interesting to note that it would only take 2,700 more people sending $30 to the losing candidate to possibly turn an election around.

Put another way, if the losing candidate, with 47% of the vote, received 185,000 votes, he or she would only have had to influence 1.5% of those voters to give another $30 to potentially turn the election around. If nothing else, this exercise should provide a glimpse into what truly motivates a member of the House.

During 2008, campaign spending, for 35 open U.S. Senate seats, totaled more than $433 million or about $12.4 million for both candidates per contest. Amazingly, some 12 Senate candidates spent more than $10 million on their campaign and, in the Minnesota race between Norm Coleman and Al

Franken, a whopping $47 million was spent between the two candidates. In all Senate races, about 66 million Americans casted votes meaning a Senator's seat costs about $6.56 per vote. Although this is slightly less per vote than a House seat, a Senator has to campaign throughout an entire State as opposed to the smaller House districts.

In the 2008 election, Presidential campaign spending totaled $1.596 billion. Just over 125.26 million voters threw the lever for one of the two major Presidential candidates translating to a cost of $12.75 per vote.

Nearly $3 billion was spent for all national offices during the 2008 election. It has become routine for various Senate and House members to bring legislation before their respective bodies aimed at limiting campaign spending and, in particular, campaign contributions from political organizations or corporations. The enormity of the cost, now counted in billions of dollars, certainly gets attention.

They demonize political actions groups and corporations who really, really spend the money on campaigns and who's spending, as of this writing, is no longer limited as a result of the Supreme Court's decision on January 21, 2010. The Court, in *Citizens United v Federal Election Commission*, voted 5-4 that, "government may not suppress political speech on the basis of the speaker's corporate identity." In short, they ruled that organizations are to be treated as though they were *individuals*. Many fear this will unleash the vast resources of corporations and trade unions to influence votes.

Consider whether or not the following questions are objectively relevant. First, has anyone really considered just how cheap American votes are? The most expensive office in America is that of the President and our votes in 2008 cost just $12.75 each and that is paid only every four years! House and Senate seats are just over half that amount. Perhaps Americans ought to raise the price for their vote.

Think about this: In reality Americans don't even get the benefit of campaign spending. We all know that the money is spent on campaign ads that keep a few hundred consultants employed and clog our favorite TV programs with vapid commercials during which most of us visit the toilet. Worse still, Americans, through taxation, are actually paying for the privilege of having our representatives spend half of their term campaigning and the other half deceiving us with rules and procedures that allow them to vote on both sides of every issue in order to pacify an occasional protest in Washington D.C.

Rather than worrying about the $3 billion (about $10 per American) spent on the 2008 campaign, maybe Americans ought to think about the $2 trillion just added to the federal deficit and a national debt that just crept over $12 trillion. If that debt was paid tomorrow, all Americans would have to pay $40,000 each. Since it would be impossible for every American to come up with that amount tomorrow the interest on the debt will continue to grow. If all 300 million Americans wanted to just make interest payments and the interest costs were to remain forever at 6%, it would still take $200 per month per American (men, women and children) just to pay the interest on the national debt. Is America getting its money's worth from the President and the 535 legislators sitting in Washington D.C.?

The nation stands at a crossroad. The division of Americans between the political left and right has never been so dramatic. The nation started with two fairly agreeable theologies, self-faith individualism and the Christian theology that places faith in God. The former pursued capitalism for the personal benefits it clearly provided and the latter pursued capitalism because it helped harness and positively direct greed.

However, capitalism produced exactly what it always does. It produced enormous economic growth but the rewards of that growth also created small minorities of extremely wealthy but powerful citizens and another small minority of extremely poor and powerless citizens composed of an inordinate percentage of minorities.

Although the nation's leaders were clearly aware of this development it took a few generations for the despair of the poor to reach their conscience. Slowly, but methodically, regulations were put into place that maintained reasonable economic growth while social programs were introduced to provide assistance to people who lived in persistent poverty.

This assistance has generally followed a path of providing equal opportunity to those who have suffered historic inequities or inequities that were fostered by prejudice. Frustrated by the lack of economic development among the poor and the growth of the poor class in America, new social agendas are being proposed that now seek to guarantee equality of *results* more than simply equality of opportunity.

How has America drifted into the current situation where the left and right seem unable to find any common ground? The answer is simple even though it has taken several generations of Americans to bring that answer into focus. The nation has seen a large portion of its population drift into a wholly different theology. Meanwhile, a roughly equal portion appears to be following the precepts of its original founders but can't, through ignorance, come close to articulating what that belief structure is.

During the last 60 years the left in America has drifted over to a subtly different theological belief. That change gradually occurred through economic policy changes introduced during and since Lyndon Johnson's presidency. He introduced new social measures under what he coined the "Great Society" program. It was intended to and succeeded in following the footsteps of Franklin Roosevelt's "New Deal." Since then social programs and Government bureaucracies have continuously expanded while a new, and mostly unproven, theory of economics has emerged as a front-running choice of social liberals.

For the last 20 years in particular, social liberals have methodically moved the entire country toward an economic policy that will ultimately replace both of America's founding theologies with something slightly different for self-faith Americans but dramatically different for those who adopt a Christian theology. The dramatic difference has arrested the attention of those who have traditional Christian beliefs, moving a few to join the choir of the religious right, but, honestly, most have sat quietly wondering what exactly happened.

The slight difference for self-faith Americans was the shift into the belief that mankind is inherently "good." It wasn't as if self-faith individuals automatically thought mankind was "bad." It's just that, at the nation's founding, there wasn't (and still isn't) any historical evidence to the contrary. The belief that mankind is inherently good is appealing on its face. It even seems rational particularly when the practice of this theology (it's religion) drives programs that provide assistance to the "needy" even though it's clearly at the expense of those whose needs have been met and exceeded through capitalism.

It isn't as if this theology, the idea that man is inherently "good," hasn't been tested. It doesn't even require a prolonged historical search to see its folly. For nearly everyone it only takes the memory required to recount the past week's events or the time to read a newspaper. There will be those who point out, with intellectual honesty, that it's not fair to paint all of mankind as "bad" based only on the actions of a few. This is a compelling argument because its underlying appeal is to fairness. But if mankind is inherently "good," fairness has no definition. What can "fair" mean if there is not a higher good than man?

Some will point out they didn't say that mankind was the "highest" good or even perfect, just good. Cutting to the chase in this argument is easy. For those who simply cannot believe there is a being above man that defines "goodness," it can be granted that mankind is "good" in general as long as the man (or woman) making the argument accepts the stipulation that some men or women are "good-er". That is hard, if not impossible, to refute.

Christian theology is very clear and precise in stating that variations of "goodness" will inevitably lead those less "good" individuals to pursue ends that come into conflict with the ends pursued by "better" individuals. In that conflict which level of "good" will be chosen? If two "good" humans cannot agree on what is best, how can we expect 535 leaders in Washington and the President to find the "good" for all 300 million Americans?

It would be so nice if America was just divided in half over this issue. It isn't. Each side of the current economic policy debate is fractured as well. The Republican Party supposedly finds limited Government (and greater capitalistic freedom) as its unifying principle. For three decades the party's fiscal conservatives have functioned in an on-again-off-again romance with its "Religious Right." It has always been a relationship of convenience for the fiscal conservatives who prefer social liberalism when it comes to questions of moral behavior.

It's a bit too simplistic to presume all Republicans have steadfastly identified with one camp or the other. Members of the "Religious Right" tend to hold the line on the moral ideals of Christian theology with strong emphasis on economic policies that acknowledge the flawed nature of humanity and support capitalism. Fiscal conservatives (sometimes referred to as the "Northeastern elites" or "Rockefeller Republicans") in the Party welcome that support and go out of their way to flame the romance up until they try to move beyond kissing and hugging and head to "second base." "Second base" is support for social policy intended to keep the Party's tent large enough to guarantee long-term power.

While Ronald Reagan was not part of this group (in fact, they initially mocked his candidacy) he surprised everyone by winning the nomination away from their preferred candidate, George H.W. Bush (from Connecticut), and won a landslide victory over a sitting President (Jimmy Carter). Analysts soon realized that Reagan won a significant Democratic cross-over vote in the South among fiscal conservatives in that Party who were becoming alarmed at the growth and intrusions of the Federal Government and among Democrat Christians, partly mobilized by the Moral Majority, who found the creeping moral ambiguity of the Democrat Party troubling. Reagan's pro-life stance won some of them over against Carter's dodgy embrace of the Democratic Party's official pro-choice position. It also didn't help Carter who, as Commander in Chief, allowed the Iranian Hostage Crisis to languish through one military foul up after another.

By the time Reagan's second term was concluding the Moral Majority's influence was waning. George H.W. Bush garnered enough support from his base among the Party's Rockefeller wing which, when added to Reagan's endorsement, kept the Republicans in command of the oval office. His infamous tax increase split the party's two wings, collapsed the "big tent," limited him to a single term, and allowed Bill Clinton to win the Presidency.

After two Clinton terms that were chronically interrupted by various ethical investigations surrounding alleged financial and moral misdeeds the Republican Party was ready to launch another big tent run at the Presidency. This time, Bush's son, George W. Bush, maintained both a fiscally conservative agenda and a high-profile profession of Christian faith and generally seemed to "walk the talk."

His popularity soared immediately following the 9/11 crisis. He committed himself to a course of pursuing a war on terrorism – regardless of where that terrorism existed. His moral commitment to the principles of Christian theology, however, wasn't matched with an equally committed supervision of what his Party was doing in the House and Senate. Over his two terms in office, Bush launched the war on terrorism on two fronts – first in Afghanistan and then in Iraq. In spite of deficit spending to fund the wars Congress, first controlled by Republicans and then by Democrats, continued to spend more and more on social programs. While the economy struggled and was temporarily stimulated by tax cuts, Congress failed to properly oversee and address the growing Mortgage crisis and it erupted into a full blown catastrophe on the eve of the 2008 Presidential election campaign.

The Republicans had nominated John McCain, a candidate that enjoyed strong support from the Party's Rockefeller wing but tepid support from the Party's religiously motivated voters. Many doubted McCain's commitment to limiting Government growth, no one thought he was remotely theologically literate, and a left-leaning media caricatured his running mate, Sarah Palin, as a dim-witted small-time Governor who had little intellectual substance – political or theological. In spite of the media's view of Palin, she drew huge crowds throughout the campaign and continued to do so even after losing the election.

Not only did Republicans lose the oval office the Democrat majorities in both houses of Congress widened giving Senate Democrats a filibuster-proof majority. Republicans immediately entered into therapy. Although, as of this writing, they remain mostly unified in a tenuous minority, the Party has awakened to a clarion call to make up its mind whether it will live to support less-socializing forms of socialism or return, even if in the minority forever, to its conservatism based on the fundamentals of Christian theology. It was Abraham Lincoln who, referencing the words of Christ, said, "A nation divided against itself cannot stand." Republicans have proved it applies to political parties as well.

What of Democrats? With overwhelming majorities in both houses of Congress and a sitting President the Party should be more unified than ever. It is not. In spite of its position the Party nearly failed to pass the centerpiece of President Obama's legislative agenda – Healthcare Reform. It was only through the rare and dubious device of congressional reconciliation that they passed the legislation without a single Republican vote. Among Democrats a different but no less strident divide exists. The division, like the Republican Party's, is all about theology at its most fundamental level. The hard left of the Party has, since the days of Franklin Roosevelt, dreamed of a utopian State where all the things contained in Maslow's hierarchy of needs become Constitutional rights.

This group is married to the idea that humanity is not just "good" but "supremely responsible" for promulgating what is "good" for everyone and everything throughout the known universe. This branch of the Democrat Party, without historical or scientific precedent, cedes mankind the responsibility – and authority – for the global economy, the global (even universal) ecology and ultimately, the global society of humans and animals. Indeed, so strong is their affinity to all things global, they seek to make all human behavior acceptable on the grounds that is – human.

If it is a given that humanity is essentially "good" what human act can be subjected to judgment? When seen in writing, here and now, the ideas seem rather extreme. Yet, these ideas are openly fostered throughout the world among those who have not only rejected the idea of a supreme being but granted themselves a moral superiority beyond that which nothing greater can be conceived.

Conservative and religious Christians are often described as "self-righteous" and arrogant. They are routinely portrayed in movies and television as ignorant, often red-neck, hicks whose beliefs are simply superstitious ramblings based on caveman-like mythology. While Christianity is founded on a long history of consistently accurate texts dating back over two millennia that record the actions and intentions of their God in the midst of historically accurate events and places, the religion of Communism is based on the deep thoughts of an admittedly learned man who lived and died during the 19th Century. And think of this: if Christians are "self-righteous," how much more are those who place their faith in themselves alone? Aren't they, by definition, more "self-righteous?"

There is no historical veracity to Communism's economic results and the clinical theories upon which it bases its philosophical, psychological and religious truth have never achieved wide acceptance and longevity in any corner of the world. Its adherents here in America, mostly found in the ultra-liberal wing of the Democrat Party, tell the world that their ideas will work but haven't yet because *they* haven't been given the chance to manage the process. It's just another way of saying they are better managers than Lenin, Stalin, Khrushchev, Brezhnev, and even Gorbachev.

Meanwhile there remains a group within the Democrat Party that has not yet opted to drink the religious Kool-Aid. These Democrats have constituents who stubbornly hold on to traditional American values even if they do not claim theology as motivation. Experiences, both good and bad, as well as a keen eye to history give them a "gut feeling" that things haven't been that bad in America. Perhaps they travel abroad and see the results of socialism there. It is also true that some Democrats dearly hold Christian theological views with limited exceptions that permit them to conscientiously support a pro-choice position when considering the legalization of abortion.

Then there are those pro-life Democrats who simply believe the Government needs to take over certain elements of the economy without going fully into socialism. Together, these Democrats are in agreement with many conservatives regarding Obama's enormous Health Care agenda. Together these Americans make up the nearly 60% who want the Health Care Bill repealed.

The far left of the Democrat Party, its leaders and President Obama, have become so committed to a socialist agenda they are continuing to press a legislative agenda of dubious constitutionality to force their version of immigration reform on a nation where national polls indicate more than 55% of voters think the Arizona immigration law should be adopted in their own State. At the time this is being written, Eric Holder, the nation's Attorney General, has filed suit in Federal Court against the State of Arizona claiming its law encroaches on the Federal Government's right to control immigration policy and enforcement.

If this drama is representative of the lines of division in America it would appear that approximately one-third of the nation hopes for a sea-change in economic policy toward socialism, one-third of the nation hopes for a return to fiscal conservatism, and the rest of the nation finds themselves in the middle and somewhat frustrated with the political party with which they have traditionally identified. In spite of the mainstream media's attempt to paint Tea Party activists as extreme and on the fringe of the political right, polls have clearly indicated that the group is made up of large numbers of citizens from both political parties. They are holding the high ground.

# LEADERSHIP

In terms of the American public, leadership is acknowledged in retrospect. Patriotism remains strong in this nation in spite of the fact that patriotic events in its history are often watered down in the text books of our public schools. For example, wedging nearly 250 years of history into a readable text book (assuming high-school students actually read their text books) is difficult to say the least, let alone trying to give each episode some historical context without political commentary ruining the soup. In the interest of political correctness the actual political context of historic events has been sanitized.

It's remarkable, really, that Americans still rally around some fundamental principles that are uniquely "American." In crisis, Americans tend to drop party affiliations (at least temporarily) and unite around the deeply held beliefs that have remained consistent throughout our history. One of those beliefs is in the dignity of the Presidential Office. Regardless of who occupies that office, Americans still tend to show a modicum of respect if for no other reason than the "Office" still peacefully passes from one President to another within two terms at the most.

It's understandable that some who lived through the 20 years previous to this writing (1990 – 2010) will recall the bruising treatment Bill Clinton received as Congress voted to make formal impeachment charges before the Senate. For his part, George W. Bush was pilloried by the mainstream media for his unique articulation of the English language. History, however, cannot be judged by a single period amounting to less than ten percent of a nation's total history. For the most part, America has enjoyed reasonably consistent leadership quality in the Presidential Office and the history written 100 years from now will likely reflect that.

Like most nations, America tends to focus attention on certain historical leaders more than others. From primary school through high school graduation, four or five Presidents are routinely singled out for their remarkable leadership skills and American textbooks uniformly put the best shine possible on those few historic leaders. George Washington, Abraham Lincoln, and Franklin Roosevelt are three that will forever receive mostly positive "press" coverage for many generations to come. (The author has to admit, however, that FDR may yet fall in favorability if America returns to a revitalized capitalistic bent).

These men have become icons. Their images are stamped on our currency and their legacies are sustained by fantasized imaginations collected and passed down through our generations. This collection of air-brushed memory forms the backdrop for our expectations of the "Office" and all other Presidents are expected to somehow measure up to that expectation. Of course, few can and even fewer do.

What characteristics of leadership do Americans admire most? It's an interesting question and, no doubt, any American could quickly jot down a list of characteristics they would prefer in their President. Superficial characteristics like a person's appearance do make a difference. Perhaps it shouldn't but history points to trends that are difficult to shake.

Washington was tall as was Lincoln. Many Presidents were physically handsome as well. Others, Lincoln for example, was certainly not considered handsome in a traditional sense but somehow carried themselves well enough to be a "presence" people noticed. Now that television has reached "high definition," the American public routinely comments on how candidates look. An open-mike comment by California Senate hopeful Carly Fiorina (R) dressed down her opponent, Senator Barbara Boxer (D), for having a "bad hair" day.

What about the character issue? Do Americans care about a leader's character? That debate raged on and on during the Clinton presidency; His romantic adventures made it into prime-time news reports. Richard Nixon resigned in embarrassment when his character was tarnished. Looking back on that time the nation was probably as alarmed by the language he used as by the deeds that made his resignation necessary.

If America, as it has been historically perceived, is going to survive this current crisis of faith it will probably require a President who is able to intellectually understand and effectually communicate the basis of our founding and motivate Americans to return to its theological roots. Even if the nation continues to drift away from its theological roots into a new era of humanism it will still take an intelligent and articulate President to shepherd that change. If the nation goes down that path the President will, more than likely, be an attractive and charismatic individual as well. Moving America in that direction will require the expert use of symbolism because the substantial argument will not hold intellectual or theological water.

In hope that America returns to its roots, what does Christian theology have to say about the character of leadership? There is no need, nor is this the medium, to go into a deep theological discourse using Scripture as support. That is certainly useful but it has been covered in great detail in books written by others. The following characteristics of leadership should be self-authenticating to anyone regardless of their individual theological beliefs. At the same time, each would pass biblical muster.

1. The greatest strength of a leader is evidenced by their willingness to serve others.
2. Leaders are not afraid to get counsel from others; they seek it, hear it, internalize its meaning and credit its sources when they use it.
3. Leaders ask the third, fourth and, sometimes, the fifth question. It's not enough to hear the standard answers prepared by the staff. Leaders probe beyond the tactical and into the realm of strategic thinking.
4. Leaders continue to think even when they're speaking.
5. Leaders do not avoid conflict; they settle it.
6. Leaders answer questions. When a question has a presupposition that's not true, they surface the presupposition, shoot it down, rephrase the question, and then answer it without ambiguity.
7. Leaders do not circumvent truth, they embrace it.
8. Leaders know they don't know everything and aren't afraid to say, "I don't know."
9. Leaders delegate; they don't abdicate.
10. Leaders train protégés and enjoy their achievements.
11. Leaders understand the concept of a budget.

12. Leaders know that borrowing is just another way to say "I've failed to find investors."
13. Leaders read more, with a wider range of genres, than their three closest advisors.
14. Leaders know how to act in public.
15. Leaders know (or learn) how to ballroom dance.
16. Leaders will instinctively seek to serve other leaders before serving themselves.
17. Leaders show deference to elder relatives, respect to their siblings or cousins and are the first to play with the kids.
18. Leaders may enjoy a drink but don't drink to enjoy.
19. Leaders aren't afraid to ask or answer the question, "Does this make me look fat?"
20. Leaders pray in public.
21. Leaders hold hands with their spouse when no one is watching.
22. Leaders mourn the passing of adversaries.
23. Leaders aren't afraid to die.
24. Leaders admonish subordinates in private.

# THE REAL LEADERS ON THE RIGHT

Presidential and congressional leaders throughout the nation's history have enjoyed a relative amount of insulation from public opinion. It is one of several unfortunate realities that, even in a democratic republic, widely disseminating political information cannot guarantee wide readership or viewership. In terms of openness and transparency, America is clearly the most transparent nation in the world.

Even though millions of Americans take the opportunity to stay abreast of political issues that concern them, the Government still manages to escape *effectual* criticism because even millions of Americans can be insignificant compared to the much larger percentage of Americans who simply do not know or care about what is going on at any given moment in time. This is not something the Government can correct. It is only something individual Americans can change.

One of the most remarkable changes in the American conversation over the past 25 years has been the impact of "talk-radio." In 1949 the Federal Communications Commission (FCC) introduced the "fairness doctrine." It was developed to assure that broadcast license holders aired issues of public concern and did so in a way that provided fairness in terms of including opposing views. However, in 1987, during the Reagan Administration, the FCC abolished the doctrine suggesting instead that the policy needed to have legislative authority either by law or through a mandated policy at the FCC.

Since that time, broadcast companies have seized on a unique phenomenon. Radio broadcast companies, for example, struggled to remain profitable as television and alternate media options curbed their profits. They found that, unimpaired by the requirement to air opposing views, they could gain audiences in sufficient number to return to commercially viability. Radio broadcasting companies experienced a sudden and remarkable financial turnaround. Whereas AM radio stations were struggling to make daytime radio shows viable they quickly latched onto national personalities who were syndicating their unique formats. Within a few months some of these personalities enjoyed national audiences numbering in the tens of millions across syndications as large as 600 stations.

One radio personality quickly dwarfed all competition. Rush Limbaugh, the self-proclaimed "doctor of democracy," emerged as the single most impactful political force on the radio. Hundreds of radio personalities attempted to jump aboard his bandwagon. The formula for success, however, wasn't immediately understood. Within a few years a handful of national radio hosts managed to emerge as high profile figures. Two features of successful shows came into clear focus. One was not hard to understand – the personality of the show's host. As always, people enjoyed listening to enjoyable and entertaining people. The other feature, however, surprised everyone – particularly America's political left.

Lulled to intellectual slumber between 1949 and 1987 (the fairness doctrine years), the left presumed that the American public would not listen to anything that wasn't inherently "fair." In fact, the outrageous nature of the most successful radio shows was met with incredulity with the left initially calling listeners' intellectual capacities into question. The left first attacked the listeners and only later launched attacks on the radio hosts themselves. In spite of numerous attempts to launch their own set of personalities the left reached the disappointing conclusion that America's radio listeners generally preferred listening to politically conservative hosts.

Ratings for talk radio are routinely gathered, using *Arbitron* data, by *Talker's Magazine.* Data from September 9th, 2009 shows that the top four, and seven of the top nine talk-radio shows, feature political discussion. Of the seven politically active talk show hosts in this group, four (Rush Limbaugh, Sean Hannity, Mark Levin and Laura Ingraham) are self-proclaimed conservatives. Two, Michael Savage and Glenn Beck, while clearly not liberal, maintain some distance from mainline republicanism. The seventh political host, Neal Bortz, is a self-proclaimed Libertarian but is generally critical of liberal policies except those in support of personal freedoms.

Bortz has an audience 1/5 the size of Rush Limbaugh's. In other words, the audience of radio hosts drops by 80% from Limbaugh to Bortz. Depending on the source, the top liberal talk show host's ratings range from 10th place to 13th. Regardless of which rank one uses, the audience size of the top liberal talker is insignificant compared to the powerful accumulation of the top conservative talkers.

The point of this departure into America's radio listening habits is to illustrate that the most articulate and convincing spokespersons for conservatism in America are on the radio rather than serving in Government. Limbaugh is routinely asked by members of his audience to throw his hat into the ring for the Presidency. His answer is nearly always the same; "I don't want to take the pay cut." Those who frequently listen to him and follow Limbaugh's career also know that he is a lightning rod for conservatism's most cherished ideals and has, for that reason alone, very high negatives (percentage of Americans who personally despise him *along with his views*). He would be too difficult to elect.

The stridency of the dialogue on conservative talk shows ultimately eliminates most, if not all, of the other popular hosts from consideration as well. Although many of the most popular conservative hosts engage in direct political activity (encouraging activism in one way or another) Limbaugh fastidiously avoids that. On just two occasions has he given out the phone numbers to the Congress or White House and urged listeners to call. The first time was just to demonstrate to doubters that his audience could shut the lines down. They did. The second time was over Speaker of the House, Nancy Pelosi's attempt to pass controversial Health Care Reform through a dubious process called "self-executing legislation" or in House jargon, "deem and pass." Limbaugh's listeners lit up the Congressional phone lines and may have prompted Pelosi to ultimately take a different strategy in passing the controversial legislation.

Given the ratings of conservative talk radio, and the fact that the top hosts don't generally compete against each other in the same time slots, it's a safe bet that between 20 and 30 million Americans **routinely** listen to one or more of these conservative talkers. Some, like Sean Hannity and Glenn Beck, also appear on television but again that audience may include many of the same Americans who listen on the radio.

Republican Presidential candidate, John McCain, had over 58 million votes in the 2008 election. Throughout the primary campaign Limbaugh heavily criticized McCain and, during the election cycle, often pointed to McCain's lack of credibility among Republicans who were both fiscally and socially conservative (the hard right) like those who made up the bulk of the Moral Majority in the 1980's and Limbaugh's audience. At one time during the primary contest Focus on the Family founder, James Dobson, vowed he would never endorse McCain. He relented on October 22, 2008, about two weeks before the election, and endorsed him. Limbaugh's support of McCain was just about as late and certainly just as tepid. McCain lost.

Conservative talk radio has demonstrated that there are men and women in America (though very few in number) who can cogently articulate conservative principles so skillfully that audiences will pay to hear them. It has also revealed there are very few Republican leaders with the intellectual capacity and oratory skills to match them.

It's true that these talk show hosts operate in a comfortable studio without the glare of klieg lights and an ornery press peppering them with questions. But they entertain and convince, in some cases, for four hours each and every day on live radio. The quality of their articulation and the soundness of their arguments are sometimes better understood when reading transcripts of their shows. Within time segments of less than six minutes, political speeches more poetic and impressive than State of the Union addresses happen on a daily basis.

Anyone that has taken the time and energy to broadly read the writings of America's founders – who has muddled their way through often complex sentences – marvels at the intellectual capacity and logical integrity with which they wrote. They were learned men. Contrast that to the drivel heard on the steps of the nation's Capitol whenever any member of our House steps in front of multiple microphones clustered atop the proverbial podium placed just seconds before their "impromptu" speech. Prepared statements that clearly obfuscate issues are read; they aren't even capable of simply speaking directly into the cameras extemporaneously about bills they've ostensibly spent months to pass. During the Health Care Bill debates it also became painfully clear that our representatives did not even read the bill they passed.

Worse, these members of our House rapidly walk away from the same podium as if the microphones were snakes waiting to strike. Press members hurriedly follow them up the steps into the Capitol building asking questions. Occasionally a member will stop to "thoughtfully" answer a question. It becomes all too apparent, however, that this too is staged as the member answers while staring off to the left or right like a kindergartner reciting their "part" of *Paul Revere's Ride.*

During the 2008 Presidential campaign millions of Americans marveled at then Senator Obama's oratorical skills. His demeanor was polished, his delivery superb and his message (though largely filled with platitude) compelling. It was soon learned that he heavily relied on a teleprompter. A recent exclusive interview (Obama's first such one-on-one as President) conducted by Fox News' Bret Baier, revealed an even more fearful prospect. The President was clearly unable to directly answer a single question or calmly surface presuppositions in Baier's questions which he possibly could have refuted. Worse still, it became increasingly clear that Baier knew more about the subject matter than the President himself. Does anyone in Government have the rudimentary conversational skills to coherently discuss policy? Isn't it ironic that these same politicians question the intellectual capacity of talk radio listeners?

There was one other element in that interview that was disturbing. At several points the President appeared to be indignant at having to answer anything. The relatively youthful look of Baier, something that he, given his responsibilities, no doubt struggles to overcome, seemed to heighten the President's discomfort. He was visibly perturbed whenever Baier tried to return his wavering attention to the *point* of a previous question.

Baier was also able to see the President's attempt to answer with deflections that served to move the discussion into areas *he* wanted to cover. The President kept saying, "Let me finish, Bret," but it was clear that the President's motivation was to continuously reframe the fundamental debate away from Baier's underlying contentions. Rather than simply acknowledging a conflict and settling it, the President wanted to act as if the basis of the conflict was immaterial.

Americans want leadership and they are finding it in a group of people who don't' hold office but who do carry out society's debates. Fox News, available only through cable, has also enjoyed a rapidly growing audience. Stylistically, they acknowledge conflicts in policy by stating both sides with intellectual clarity and clearly identify pundits who comment as left or right proponents. The mainstream media, meanwhile, treats adverse opinions as "news" which they then marginalized using sound bites from the left.

Professional salespersons (not necessarily an oxymoron) know that purchase decisions are made on emotion but justified with logic. It is one reason car commercials don't spend a lot of time pointing out the details of their warranty program. Instead they use images that evoke feelings of freedom, success, fun and sexual power. In one notable commercial, Kate Walsh, the sexy Grey's Anatomy actress, drives her new Cadillac CTS in a slinky dress and high heels making this statement, "...the real question is: When you turn your car on, does it return the favor?"

In a society where there is no baseline morality, or ethical mandate that is considered universally true, individuals will generally opt to do whatever "feels" best. What feels best isn't just sensory pleasure either. Humanity, whether liberal, conservative or something in between, learns through experience that sensory joys don't happen in a vacuum. If they did, there would be no meaning to the phrase, "The morning after."

The ethical model that is historically built around pleasure was first posited by Epicurus and those who hold to its model in modern times are usually called Epicureans. The model seeks to find the balance of pleasure and pain in personal license tempered by moderation. People who live with nothing but momentary pleasure as their objective are generally considered hedonists.

As individuals join social groups the pleasure principle is further modified to provide that one's personal pleasure shouldn't inflict pain on others. Once the social group grows to the point of requiring behavior standards that mutually benefit everyone things get more complicated but not immediately chaotic.

Libertarians, for example, do not attempt to achieve personal freedom at the expense of others but do seek to enjoy the freedom to act in any way that has no impact whatsoever on others. The test for the impact on others varies from one libertarian to another but it's safe to say that libertarians won't encourage the regulation of drug use or other behaviors when the damages are limited to the user. Libertarians run into problems, however, when societies question whether anything one human does can, in fact, have no impact on others.

The point is that a society that does not have a broadly accepted concept of right and wrong will experience conflict between competing ideas of morality held by individuals living in that society. If in that society moral standards continue to be subjective, actions will be rationalized logically after the fact. Individuals will "shoot first and ask questions later." Furthermore, individuals will have a strong tendency to raise the intensity of a dispute as opposed to reinforcing their argument because there may not be enough objective agreement on just what is actually right and wrong.

In popular parlance the Democrat Party is known as the "party of the little guy." The party's history is steeped in being the place where the underdog will find strength in numbers through the coalition of various "oppressed" groups. In terms of race, the 2008 Presidential election results indicated the strength of the Democrats among minorities; 96% of African-Americans, 63% of Asian-Americans and 67% of Latino-Americans voted for President Obama. In terms of labor union membership, CNN exit polls indicated that 61% of self-identified union members voted by President Obama. The same exit poll revealed that 86% of non-white voters with household incomes below $50,000 voted for President Obama while 60% of all voters with household incomes below $50,000 voted for him. In terms of religion, Protestants (at 54%) voted for Senator John McCain. Catholics, Jews, those who are self-proclaimed as non-religious or joined to other religions voted for President Obama by percentages ranging from 54% (Catholics) to as high as 78% (Jews). 70% of those self-identified as "gay or lesbian" voted for Obama.

Whether it is household income, race, union membership, religion or sexual preference, the Democrat Party attempts to represent America's various minorities and, historically, continues to enjoy support from all those groups. The coalition of these interest groups is held together by an emotional bond; it is the party's commitment to harness its various minorities into a powerful majority. That majority's mandate is to ensure equality of opportunity for all of its oppressed groups. In order to maintain the strength of its numbers, however, Democrats illogically promise to achieve equal outcomes because equal opportunity alone cannot hold their coalition together.

However, equal outcomes can only be realized if a nationwide majority simply presumes the essential "goodness" of humanity. Since that can't be proved logically and is diametrically opposite of an underlying tenet of Christianity, it must be sold through emotionally charged images of "oppression" along with an appeal to a moral sense of what "good" people ought to do. The irony is that these images exactly express the historical evidence that mankind, whether operating individually or in congress with others, is not "good" at all.

But, proving the "goodness" of humanity is virtually impossible in terms of logical dialectic. It can be presumed by inference only if there is no objective basis (a higher good) from which to pass judgment on humanity. Proving that mankind is "bad", while not without historical precedent, is likewise difficult because it also has to be presumed based on the possibility that something or someone higher than mankind establishes that which is ultimately "good" and therefore a base from which to measure mankind's behavior.

So, both viewpoints rest on faith; only those who place their faith in that beyond which nothing greater can be conceived can and do provide rational support to their view using historical precedent. Self-faith proponents, lacking historical precedent, have no choice but to make emotional appeals aimed at moving America's populace toward empathy for those individuals who are said to be "less fortunate" than they. This emotion, however, presumes that the "fortunate" achieve results through nature's lottery rather than through individual effort.

The national debate over reforming America's health care system illustrates this reality. The supporting evidence could be seen in the House of Representatives where every Republican representative, joined by 34 Democrats, voted against HR 3590 (The Senate Health Care Bill passed in December of 2009).

Those who witnessed the debate itself on Sunday, March 21st, 2010, were treated to ample support for the strength of emotional arguments. One poster, used by Democrat representatives during several speeches, said, "45,000 Americans die each year because they have no health insurance." The statement's "logical" conclusion is predicated exclusively on the presupposition that simply having health insurance would miraculously prevent all illness-related deaths in America.

The arguments in support of nationalizing health care ultimately depended on what the nation "ought" to do. Democrats presented examples of individual constituents (by definition a minority) who suffer because they lacked either proper health care or health insurance. Each example, while compelling, rested on the presupposition that the Government ought to intervene to guarantee equal outcomes in life. How can anything be condensed to an "ought" when there is no moral absolute upon which that "ought" is defined? What can prevent a majority of the "less fortunate" from simply declaring what "fortunate" Americans ought to do?

It would be intellectually disingenuous to claim that all members of the Democrat Party based their sense of what ought to happen in America on the wishes of minorities. Many find their motivation comes from a different, perhaps more substantial, ethical foundation that has broad acceptance in America.

Many Americans find ethical "oughts" expressed through religious mandates. Although this group is difficult to measure in terms of percentage it can be generically described as those Americans who adhere to what are called Judeo-Christian ethics and would encompass a large segment (perhaps even a majority) of America's population.

These ethics are variously derived from precepts contained in the Bible. For some in this group it is not considered essential to believe that mankind is inherently flawed – even though that is uniformly expressed throughout the Bible. Instead, ethical behavior is based on the belief that there is a God (the God of the Bible) and that mankind, as a creation of God, must adhere to His law in order to benefit from the law's goodness in opposition to anything mankind, as a creature, could rise to or imagine on its own.

The "Ten Commandments," for example, expressed God's mandate for social order and were established as law for the Hebrew nation. They were considered inherently "good" by virtue of their source. The Hebrew King, David, wrote of these inherent qualities saying, "The law of the LORD is perfect...the statutes of the LORD are right...the commandment of the LORD is pure...the judgments of the LORD are true and righteous altogether." (Psa. 19:7-9)

The social value of these commandments has been accepted into cultures and nations beyond the original Hebrew recipients. Moses holding the commandments is even displayed in sculpted reliefs atop the United States Supreme Court building. It is not at a stretch to state there is broad agreement that these laws are universally adoptable excepting perhaps the first commandment to have no other gods other than the God of the Bible and the second which was a law against idolatry.

The Judeo-Christian ethic incorporates the totality of law as expressed in the Bible which includes the Ten Commandments, the ancillary laws developed throughout the Hebrew exodus and the laws of love expressed in the teachings of Jesus. Together these laws have found expression and practice in America's several Jewish and/or Christian religious denominations and form, at least in part, the foundation upon which our national laws rest.

Throughout the nation's history individual behavior has been restricted by society based upon the general expression of the Bible concerning what individuals ought to do and, to varying extents, those individual behaviors society must forbid. Over its 250 year history America has, however, openly welcomed other cultural and religious views into the legal melting pot that is now American law. As a result, some individual behaviors that would otherwise be "illegal" according to a biblical view have become wholly accepted alternate lifestyles. Adultery, for example, may be frowned upon but is certainly not illegal (For a view of how adultery was legally treated in colonial America you may want to read Nathaniel Hawthorne's *The Scarlet Letter*). Likewise the mandate to refrain from coveting is set aside for how else would Americans be motivated to purchase non-essential goods?

But, individual behavior mandates contained in the Bible have become quite inconvenient in America today. The social clash between biblical behavior standards and radical individualism found its most titanic battles during the 1960's. The righteous fervor of preceding generations pitted religious legalism against popular culture's icons and the battle began in earnest. As a refresher to older generations and a firsthand account to youths, some behavior standards (legalisms) commonly practiced during the middle of the last Century are listed below:

1. Children who misbehaved were routinely spanked in private *and* in public.
2. Children and young adults were expected to address elders as "sir" or "ma'am."
3. Girls or young, single, women were not to be roaming around unescorted. They were to always be accompanied by another girl or an adult.
4. Public displays of affection (especially between unmarried   couples) were considered scandalous at worst and in poor taste at best.
5. Young men were expected to act, dress and groom themselves in consistency with their fathers.
6. The use of vulgarity was strictly prohibited in mixed (male/female) company.
7. Profanity (taking God's name in vain) was an utterly appalling thing to do. It was even grounds for suspension in public school.

8. Although drinking alcoholic beverages was permitted, drunkenness was considered sinful. Prohibition had been lifted but large segments of America's Protestant population continued to believe any form of drinking alcohol was sinful. Yes, even beer was considered sinful.
9. Television programs were prohibited from showing even married couples sharing a bed (thus, Dick Van Dyke and Mary Tyler-Moore had twin beds on the Dick Van Dyke Show).
10. There was no designated hitter in baseball.

Each of these behaviors (even the designated hitter!) were based on broadly held moral values which became inconvenient when set against growing individualism and its promise of immediate gratification.

As these standards gave way to the encroachment of new individual rights, it became easier and easier to culturally abolish any standard of personal conduct. Not only are biblical standards of personal conduct completely disregarded today, outrage has been reserved for those who try to curb individual expressions that were once thought to be outrageous. Throughout most of America today it would be considered outrageous to restrict (let alone make illegal) homosexual behavior even though it is expressly (that means in writing) forbidden in both the Old and New Testaments of the Bible.

Some of the inconvenient "oughts" of the Bible are not the responsibility of the individual but of the society. American law once embraced many of these social mandates incorporating them into the law of the land. Recent cultural changes have caused America to discard a few including the right of the unborn to life, liberty and the pursuit of happiness. That right was abrogated when the Supreme Court (through judicial activism) discarded the biblical standard for life and replaced it with its own unfounded and medically unproven compromise establishing that the value of life in the womb is to be divided into trimesters during which that "life" becomes progressively human.

Likewise, the right of individuals to enjoy the fruit of their labor has increasingly come under attack through an ever expanding social agenda that can only be funded by taxing the labor of wealthy individuals. As that social agenda has expanded so has the definition of "wealthy." It has also been attacked by the new Healthcare legislation which will, for the first time in American history, force individuals to purchase something they might otherwise freely choose not to purchase – health insurance.

In the constant tug of war for attention to what America (and Americans individually) ought to do it has become clear that there is no unassailable and fundamental principle for determining what is good or bad. It cannot be based on the ideas of individuals alone as in Libertarianism. It cannot be based on the idea that mankind is inherently "good" because there is no historical accuracy supporting that assumption. It is nothing but an opinion. It also cannot be reliably placed on the "goodness" of God's laws because, mankind, true to its historically flawed nature, will find ways to circumvent God's mandates when and if they come into conflict with a culture, like America's, of immediate gratification.

What then is America to do? What will you do?

# PART FOUR

## A RETURN TO BIBLICAL LITERACY AND BELIEF

All that has been covered to this point has been descriptive of the state of affairs in America. The foundations of morality, economic policy, political and religious activity have been described. From this point forward attention will be focused on the prescription for bringing American Christians back to a sustainable unity.

If an American evangelical preacher were writing this he/she might say that America needs a revival. While revivals, historically, have had their place in shaping a nation's views the problem is evident in the word itself. It implies something that has to recur at regular intervals otherwise there would be no "re" as a prefix in the word. It conjures up a vision of the dead being brought back to life but what if that life was unproductive in the first place. In order for America to have a true revival at this point in history it must first have a life worthy of revitalizing.

Friedrich Nietzsche, a German philologist who was born in 1844 and died in 1890, is credited with writing, "God is dead." His statement was predicated on the view that scientific discovery and Europe's secularization (much like modern America's) had "killed the Christian God." He predicted that the "death" of God would lead to the collapse of universal perspective on things and objective truth. Although Nietzsche's declaration of God's death may have been premature its philosophical conclusion was spot on. Removing God from the conversation of mankind will mean the loss of objective truth and that is the condition of the world in general and America specifically. God has been removed from the dialogue because to include him, especially in political policy decisions, would ostensibly violate the Constitution's separation of church and state. Of course this is nonsense.

It is not necessary for America to become a Christian State but it may be necessary, for her long term survival, to become filled with at least a majority of Christian adherents who possess something that periodically needs to be revived. That something is theological and biblical literacy.

Before anyone can understand (let alone foster the growth of) the precepts and mandates of Christianity they must be willing to read its singularly accepted governing document – the Bible – and develop a comprehensive and internally consistent theology in keeping with its teachings. The fractious nature of Christianity in America is rooted in its various denominational practices and those practices, for the most part, arise from differing views of the accuracy, relevance and interpretation of the Bible.

It is not necessary for every American Christian to agree on all points of theological contention. Over its 2,000 year history many have tried to settle natty arguments arising from such things as a single word and its meaning. In the end nearly every one of these debates has led to an impasse or resulted in the creation of another Christian denomination. If American Christians, however, long for a sustainable bedrock from which to build economic and political policy it will be necessary to fully understand those points where believers have, through narrowed interpretation, departed from one another and fostered the abandonment of what would otherwise be mutually acceptable policy.

The question, then, is whether or not Christian Americans (and anyone else interested) have the stomach and intellectual intensity to dig into the Bible for answers. It will also be necessary for those who think of themselves as biblical scholars or experts to set aside the expectation that Americans ought to know everything they do. It would be truly wonderful if Christians returned en masse to the regular reading and study disciplines of our forefathers. Their familiarity of the Bible allowed them to communicate widely held principles with a single sentence of or allusion to a Bible story. How many times have you heard the phrase, "the writing's on the wall" but never knew it was an allusion to Scripture?

Since it is unlikely that American Christians will suddenly change their reading habits, set down the television remote, and undertake the discipline of theology, it might be useful to provide a synopsis of the Bible's content. A synopsis or general overview is useless, however, without some form of commentary. That commentary will be exclusively focused on the prescription of unifying American Christians around defensible policy conclusions. There will be points where the commentary is controversial but an honest effort will be given to provide the alternate view points with genuine respect for those who hold them. In every instance where Christians depart over principle in the commentary, one conclusion will be put forward as "best" in the interest of retaining the drive toward unity. At the end of the day it would be a monumental achievement if those reading this synopsis became inspired enough to start reading the Bible for themselves.

There is one principle taught within Scripture that bears repeating. It is the principle that Scripture itself, having its origin in God, has the power to change and direct individual lives. It would be a much greater thing, then, if one would read *it* rather than the synopsis and commentary that follow here. God should be trusted (and is) to provide insight and commentary (by His Spirit) to what is, after all, His Word.

## THE BIBLE'S STRUCTURE

Nearly everyone is familiar with the fact that the Bible is divided into what are commonly called the Old and New Testaments. Within these two parts the history of earth's beginning and God's selection of the Hebrew nation is contained in the Old Testament. The advent (appearance) of Jesus Christ, his life and teachings together with interpretive theology, make up the New Testament. Jews accept only the Old Testament as God's word while Christians claim both Testaments as God's word and believe they are both part of God's progressive revelation of himself to humanity. Having said that, too many Christians are wholly unfamiliar with the Old Testament and think the New Testament was intended to replace it and its usefulness. It doesn't. It might even surprise some Christians (particularly those people who only nominally call themselves Christians) that Jesus was a Jew. The entirety of the Gospels outline the truths Jesus sought to communicate to his own people, the Jews, within the framework of Judaism.

Throughout both Testaments, Scripture is further divided into segments according to genre or the literary style of the writing. These segments can be loosely identified as Law, History, Prophets, Poetry and Wisdom literature in the Old Testament while the New Testament can be divided into Gospels, Epistles and Prophecy. This is not to suggest that prophecies are never included in the History segment or that poems never occur in the Law. The divisions are the creation of scholars who recognize a literary style and interpretive purpose consistently used in the various segments.

The organization of the individual books of the Bible is not chronological meaning that those books written first aren't necessarily the first books one reads. Although the books within the History segment contain historical accounts it is not generally believed to be the reason the books were written. In other words it was not the aim of the writers (or God's apparent design) to make the books of history an *exhaustive* account of all history. Instead, the design was to communicate what scholars call "holy history" or the history of God's intentions regarding mankind.

Although the Bible had many writers contribute individual works, only those works which, through their accepted inclusion, are considered "inspired" and are believed to have their origin in God himself. The inspiration of God is one of the primary (perhaps most important) characteristics required for a book to be included in Scripture. There are many theories as to how God's inspiration worked in conjunction with the writers. For example, the "dictation" theory suggests that God actually verbally dictated the exact words. Others take a quite different view suggesting that the writer's own personality and talents operated in conjunction with God's sovereign will to produce something holy even though it was essentially a cooperative effort between God and man. The latter view is generally preferred because it reinforces both God's sovereign will and the free will God gave mankind when he created man "in his image." The concept elevates mankind without diminishing the character and attributes of God.

The importance of Scripture being "inspired by God" cannot be understated. The source and origin of Scripture (God) is what makes the Bible "authoritative" in terms of establishing truth in an absolute moral and ethical sense. Scripture's connection to God is the very thing that makes it *the* source of what humanity considers "good." This is not to be confused with accuracy for there are many theologians who do not consider the Bible to be wholly, 100%, accurate in every historical detail or that it contains no errors that may have occurred during the transmission of the texts through copying that took place over thousands of years.

The theology of the Bible is internally consistent. That means that, while there may be numerical inconsistencies or literary mistakes that resulted from scribal errors, the message of the text when taken in its entirety shows a consistent portrayal of God and humanity. There are theologians who, for whatever purpose known only to them, have attacked more than just the accuracy of the text. Some have called into question its literary purpose and therefore the underlying meaning of the words.

It is immeasurably safer to trust the opinion of accumulated scholarship throughout history when one attempts to find the meaning of Scripture. It is absolutely true that the most significant attacks on the meaning of Scripture have occurred during the last 50 years. Most of these attacks have the consequence of calling God's inspiration of the text into question. In other words, some scholars simply do not like what God has been previously thought to have said and therefore look for ways and means to change the meaning of the words so that an alternate interpretation will have some sense of authority.

The most common quandary when attempting to interpret Scripture is whether or not the text should be always taken literally. Beware anytime qualifiers like "always" and "never" are used for anything. Scripture is inherently complex for reasons that will be addressed in a moment. However the text itself generally provides the best information into how it should be interpreted. Parts of it are clearly literal while others are clearly allegorical.

At times Scripture is both a literal account of an historical event but simultaneously allegorical in foreshadowing other events in the future. It is important that one never interprets Scripture in a vacuum. All Scripture has context and it is vitally important that one understands the full context of a particular verse or passage. Context for a passage isn't limited to the verses before and after a particular text either. Context includes the historical events surrounding the written account. It is also safe, in the end, to use Scripture (in other passages with similar context) when interpreting Scripture instead of developing one's own presuppositions about meaning.

Now, to that part about Scripture's complexity: Whenever a person undertakes to read a work by Mark Twain that person will undoubtedly form opinions about the author based on his characterization of the people his stories involve. Just so, the Bible is not only intended to describe its characters but to communicate the attributes of its Author as well.

In fact, the Bible is, in essence, the history of God's intervention into the lives of men and women who are representative of all humanity. His intervention is progressive. That means that only through the totality of God's story can anyone truly understand his character and attributes. The organization of the individual books of the Bible help to make that progressive revelation of God understandable so that, when one has completely read all of Scripture, God's image and man's identity with God comes into view in the same way the richness of a painting is more apparent as one steps backward to take in its entirety. Likewise when one steps forward to see the mastery of the painter's individual strokes the depth of humanity's nature and God's moments of mercy come into view.

The final interpretation of Scripture cannot include one view without the other. Denominational differences have generally emerged whenever someone did just that – took a close up view of God or man without the benefit of stepping back to see the totality of God's mission. Yet, the superintendence of God over his people is such that even denominational differences rarely disrupt the principle message of the Bible. There are exceptions, of course; it would be naïve to suggest otherwise.

The greatest and most dangerous exception are those denominational views that attack the Divine attributes of God or improperly elevate the goodness of mankind. This is monumental when it comes to the person of Jesus Christ. Scripture, both Old and New Testaments together, paint the landscape of his Divinity – that he is truly God incarnated into human flesh.

## HISTORY

It is a signal act of God that he chose to demonstrate his character and attributes using something mankind universally understands – history. We may not like to study history but it is, after all, something we live through each and every day. Having created both time and space God uses time and space to help humanity comprehend what would otherwise be incomprehensible. Not only is humanity limited to the direction of time (it always goes forward) but mankind's thought process uses the totality of timely awareness to organize the meaning of life. Humans learn through experience and the concept of causes and effects have been established by the creation of time so that our behavior is gradually modified by our experiences. With that as a backdrop the story of God, beginning in Genesis, emerges.

The book of Genesis does not begin with a rational explanation of God and his origins from a human perspective even though it was the human, Moses, who is believed to have written the text. Because he was "inspired" the text begins with the presupposition that God simply exists and that his existence is independent from anything that is seen in creation. This is important for two reasons. It establishes at the outset that the Bible is not about

114

the adventures (or misadventures) of mankind. It also shows that creation itself (literally everything humanity can experience through the scientific method) came about through the agency of God's will. It establishes that God stands outside of and is therefore independent from the thing he created.

It is very interesting to note that Moses actually encountered God on Mt. Sinai. The account, in Exodus, describes how God could not allow Moses to directly see his face but that God would hide Moses in a cleft of a rock, pass by him, and hold his "hand" over the opening so that Moses could witness his presence without dying. This story could have and probably would have preceded anything in Scripture if Moses (or you or I for that matter) were writing the story without God's inspiration. Wouldn't it have been more reasonable and rational if Moses had simply written at the beginning of Genesis, "I saw God; he exists but I can't begin to describe him accurately but, what the hay, I'll try?"

Without God's oversight of its writing, the Bible would certainly have started off with an explanation that included exactly *how* God did everything. It would have attempted to describe and quantify God from our viewpoint. However, God, who is not quantifiable, did oversee the writing of Scripture because the Bible is not about our viewpoint of him but about his viewpoint of us. With God as the author humanity is graciously rewarded with a progressively revealing picture of God and his purposes for humanity. It is mysteriously devoid of explanations about "how" God accomplishes anything.

The Bible begins with God creating the universe as we currently understand it. Through intentions that are not explained, God undertakes to create a man in his own image. That is the only explanation given initially – that mankind was made in the image of God. Theologians must understand the entirety of Scripture to catalogue all the ways humanity is like God because God himself is only partially revealed within individual components of Scripture whether that is a book or an individual story. As the character and attributes of God are discerned the similarities and differences between God and man are noticed.

Upon completing the creation of a male, Adam, from the "dust of the earth," God declares that the male must not live alone but will need what God calls a "help-mate." While all the animals created to that point had a means of procreation, man without a woman would have no such capacity. It is interesting as well to note that God acknowledged that the procreation of humanity was not the only reason to create a female. God understood that humanity, without companionship, would be inherently dissatisfied. God took a portion of Adam's rib and, from it, fashioned a woman. Only after having completed the creation of Eve did God declare that it (his creation of humanity) was "good."

God elected to place the human couple into a perfect environment called the Garden of Eden. Within this environment he provided a means of sustenance and, interestingly, a singular rule. The only rule God established was that humanity was not to eat from or even touch a tree he created and called the Tree of the Knowledge of Good and Evil. God warned both Adam and Eve that they would die on the day they disobeyed that rule.

That single rule allows theologians (and you, too) to draw some pretty safe conclusions. One is that both "good" and "evil" were irrelevant terms for humanity as long as they obeyed that one and only rule. Through obedience everything could remain just as God created it – "good." There would be no need for Maslow to describe what humans seek and in what order it is sought because everything humanity needed was already available. Another conclusion was that humanity was given a choice and, importantly, the freedom to exercise it. The fact that God gave mankind choice is one reason some Christians honestly believe they can support a Pro-Choice position on Abortion. They correctly claim that God gave humanity the right to choose their own destiny. He did. However, God clearly designated that choices (like the choice in the Garden of Eden) could be either "good" or "evil." The totality of Scripture, as we will see, places an infinite and eternal value on the life of the unborn and is why most Christians are Pro-Life.

Adam and Eve's freedom of choice was soon put to a test when a new character was introduced into the garden scene. Scripture tells of a serpent who spoke to Eve telling her that God had forbid her (and Adam) from eating from the Tree of the Knowledge of Good and Evil only because he (God) knew that when they ate from the tree they would become like "gods" knowing the difference between good and evil. Adam and Eve ultimately succumbed to the temptation freely acting to achieve something they *wanted*, even though it broke God's one and only rule, rather than to have remained content with having everything they *needed*.

This is a great time to address one of Christianity's most troublesome questions. Like listening to a three-year old when they first discover that rules can be logically tested, questions come on like a torrent and usually begin with "why." Christians will ultimately encounter the question, "Why did God create evil?" Many Christians struggle mightily with this question without ever looking carefully at its underlying presupposition. The question presumes that God actually created evil when it is clear that "evil" cannot be "created."

As Scripture unfolds and the reader completes other segments it becomes clear that after God's creation of the universe, but at some time before Adam and Eve sinned, a rebellion took place in the "heavens." A singular and very highly esteemed angel, called Lucifer, was also given the freedom to choose whether or not to obey God. Evil was not created but was instead the <u>descriptive state</u> of Lucifer's existence after his disobedience. His act is the definition of those acts, among humans, which do not conform to the character and attributes of God. It (evil) is not a created "thing." It is simply the state of being in which one exists after having acted in contradiction to God's command.

Lucifer's rebellion is reported in Scripture to have included one-third of the created angels in heaven. His rebellion is described as an act to usurp the dominion of God replacing God with himself. Eve's temptation was similar. The temptation was to become like God and her act of defiance (which Adam freely joined) was the first such act among humanity and thereafter redefined the entire universe in terms of human existence. Rather than accepting the role of beloved creatures, both Adam and Eve disobeyed and disqualified themselves from all that God intended for them to enjoy.

In order to affirm his sovereignty and protect Adam and Eve, God removed them from the Garden of Eden by placing an angel at its entrance to protect it from them and, in truth, them from it. In so doing, God deprived them of its sustenance, the eternal life which came from the "Tree of Life," so they would not live forever in the fallen (evil) descriptive state disobedience brought. God further cursed the earth beginning the history of its vulnerability to entropy (the state wherein all things ultimately fail) and placed all of humanity for ages to come into a physical state that progressively declined into death.

Christians and non-Christians alike wonder whether Adam and Eve's disobedience actually affected all of humanity. They wonder how just one singular act of disobedience could result in all of humanity being "flawed." This debate is usually called the "original sin" debate. Scripture is largely silent when it comes to explaining "how" this worked but is consistent in describing humanity as sinful from birth. Israel's King David, writing poetry in the book of Psalms, said, "In sinfulness was I conceived." This was not a statement indicating that the act of procreation (intercourse) was sinful but that sinfulness somehow permeates humanity so entirely that it either universally "affects" mankind or perhaps "infects" mankind. In either case, Christian theology uniformly (among Catholics and Protestants) holds that the totality of Scripture teaches that all of humanity is either sinful at birth or that all of humanity will eventually sin through disobedience of God's commands.

God further established a principle that repentance alone could not reinstate humanity's initial "goodness" nor could it return humanity to a state where communion with God was possible. God's "holiness," the utter absence of anything evil in his character and attributes, could not allow anything less holy in his presence. This is why Lucifer was cast out of heaven. Instead God enacts the first instance of atonement. Its objective was to essentially cover over man's enmity with God (humanity's flawed condition), through a substitutional execution of an innocent animal. God ordained this sacrifice on the basis that all animals are innocent. They are incapable of sin since they have no law or rules to disobey. They also do not have free will in the sense of having the capacity to acknowledge God's will and choose to rebel against it.

Mankind was given that faculty, that ability to acknowledge God coupled with the freedom and ability to choose to disobey. In making that choice, humanity was guilty and the sentence was, in fact, death. However, God once again revealed his mercy by allowing humanity to reinstate communion with God through regular sacrifices of an innocent animal in substitution for themselves. God himself conducted the first sacrifice by killing an animal from which skins were fashioned by God to cover Adam and Eve's nakedness.

This substitutional sacrificial system was ultimately made a part of the law God gave Moses on Mt. Sinai. From Adam forward, including the time in history when the Hebrews killed lambs and placed the blood over the doors and door frames of their homes in Egypt before the night of Passover, the blood sacrifice was the only acceptable way to atone for one's sins. It should also be noted that this sacrifice merely postponed God's judgment and enactment of the duly deserved death penalty. Human life since that time until now still ends in death but the existence of the penalty and humanity's actual condition (inherently flawed) will, according to Scripture, remain until Jesus (who actually became a human substitutional sacrifice took on all of humanity's death sentences on the cross once and for all) returns to earth to relieve humanity and all creation from the curse of sin.

As Scripture moves forward from the events after creation humanity continues to exercise self determination in contradiction to God's command. Adam and Eve's first son, Cain, murders his younger brother, Abel, over (of all things) the requirement to present a blood sacrifice to God. Cain opts to sacrifice fruits and vegetables while Abel, in obedience, brings the first born from his flock. In jealousy over God's acceptance of Abel's sacrifice Cain murders Abel and hides his body.

The society of humanity grows in numbers and in continuous disobedience to the point where God, again affirming his sovereignty, elects to destroy all of humanity except Noah and his family in a worldwide flood. Saving Noah was, according to Scripture, an act of God's grace. His selection of Noah was not based on anything inherently "good" about Noah. In fact Noah proceeded to get drop dead drunk the minute he got out of the ark. Disobedience and sinfulness continued to haunt mankind even after Noah and his family started over in the replenishment of the human population.

Scripture goes on to tell that a large society grew from the family of Noah. Finding a suitable place to build a city, humanity with a common language and heritage decided to build a tower that reached to the sky. The tower was a monument to their achievements and a display they hoped would discourage anyone else from attacking them. God, once again affirmed his sovereignty by miraculously confusing their languages. Suddenly they no longer understood each other and were forced to separate into city-nations as they spread across the land.

As nations rose and fell humans began to practice religions based upon deities they either created (idols) or imagined. Idolatry was rampant and superstitions governed. In a land called Ur of the Chaldea's, God visited a man named Abram. He called Abram away from the idolatry commonly observed in his homeland and promised him that he would be led to a land called Canaan – modern day Israel.

At his calling Abram was also promised a son from whom God would establish a nation of chosen people. Abram's wife Sarai was barren and very advanced in age. In exasperation over her inability to conceive, Sarai finally opted for a then common practice of providing Abram a concubine with whom to conceive a child. Her handmaiden, Hagar, was given to Abram and she conceived giving birth to a son whom they name Ishmael. While God was unhappy that the couple chose to take things into their own hands, he reaffirmed the promise that Abram and Sarai would have their own biological son and changed their names to Abraham and Sarah as a sign of his promise. About a year later Sarah gave birth to Isaac. Abraham's two sons, Ishmael and

Isaac, went on to form competing nations whose conflicts continue to rage on today.

Ishmael's progeny developed into the northern Arabs and their religion became Islam. Islam is directly tied to the belief that Abraham's first born, Ishmael, is the rightful heir to Abraham's God-given legacy. Scripture, however, focused on Isaac and his family, particularly his son, Jacob, whom God renamed Israel. From this critical point in history to the time when Israel's second Temple was destroyed, the Bible records God's selection of Israel as a nation belonging exclusively to him and over which he will ultimately rule as "Messiah" or King Incarnate.

## THE NATIONAL HISTORY OF ISRAEL

The story of Israel, as a nation, is filled with compelling characters and heart-rending accounts of their struggles to remain faithful to God. The stories are beautiful and really need to be enjoyed and understood as they form patterns that repeat themes which lead up to the birth of Jesus and the beginning of the Christian faith. It's unfortunately necessary, since this is an overview, to summarize in very broad terms the national development of the Hebrew people. Within that development one will see a wide range of economic and political experiments in government. The underlying message is somewhat surprising in that not a single form of government ultimately endures except that a hope is forecasted in a yet to be realized Kingdom where God is King. This is shown to be the ultimate answer because of humanity's fallen nature. Every form of Government fails through the immorality of humanity.

Although God elected and renamed Jacob, the nation of Israel (Jacob's offspring) is eventually taken into slavery. Jacob prospers to the point where, in spite of vast wealth, a famine forces him to send his sons to Egypt for food. While there, his sons encounter a mysterious Prime Minister of Egypt who, as things turn out, happens to be their very own younger brother, Joseph, whom they had sold into slavery because Jacob obviously favored him over all of his sons. After selling him into slavery the brothers lied to their father telling him that Joseph had been killed by a wild beast.

In a story of redemption not unlike the kind of redemption Jesus will one day execute on behalf of humanity, Joseph rescues his family from the famine and moves them to Egypt where his wealth and power protect them until he dies. Another Pharaoh that does not know of Joseph's history struggles to keep the burgeoning Hebrew population from overtaking his country.

In an effort to control the population of Hebrews the Egyptian Pharaoh declares a policy of infanticide where all Hebrew males under the age of two are to be killed. One Hebrew family places their new born son, Moses, into a watertight basket and puts him into the Nile River where he is rescued by Pharaoh's daughter. Raised in Pharaoh's household, Moses is elevated in importance but somehow learns that he is himself a Hebrew.

He encounters an Egyptian slave driver who is mercilessly beating a Hebrew man. Enraged, Moses kills the Egyptian and is forced to leave Egypt in exile. He spends 40 years in the desert as a herdsman when one day God appears to him in the form of a bush that is burning but never consumed. God instructs Moses to return to Egypt where he is to demand that Pharaoh release the Hebrews from slavery and allow them to return to their homeland.

Through a series of negotiations punctuated by 10 plagues that God inflicts on Egypt, the tenth and last plague has God's death angel taking the lives of all of Egypt's first born sons. The Hebrew people, under instructions from Moses, kill lambs and place the blood above and on the sides of their doors just prior to the death angel's arrival. This sacrifice comes to be enshrined in Hebrew Law as the Passover.

Distressed by the loss of his own son, Pharaoh relents and allows Moses to take the entire nation away from Egypt. The journey to their promised land, however, takes a circuitous route during which God establishes a Law for the people that is given to Moses on Mt. Sinai. Throughout the journey the people chronically complain about one thing or another and Moses, in exasperation, receives advice from his father-in-law, Jethro, about how to administrate justice and govern the people. Moses establishes a kind of representative government whereby the nation is divided into twelve tribes representing the twelve sons of Jacob. Within these tribes, elders are elected to administer justice up to the point where appeals, when necessary, are taken directly to Moses for final judgment. Bear in mind that it was a man (Jethro) rather than God who suggested this representative form of governance. God himself establishes the administration of his Law through a Priesthood led by Moses' brother, Aaron. The priesthood includes the tribe of Levi and also consists of the first born sons among the other tribes.

Because of a particularly egregious act of disobedience on the part of Moses, he is not allowed, ultimately, to enter into the Promised Land. The nation crosses the Jordan River into Canaan under the leadership of Moses' protégé, Joshua. Under commandment from God, Joshua leads the armies of Israel in a lengthy process to purge the land of idolatry and idolatrous nations. This effort is never completely successful and Israel is persistently attacked by competing Nations and competing theologies. The most serious theological threat, for many generations, is the idolatrous worship of a god called Baal.

When Joshua and the entire generation of Israelites who experienced the journey into Canaan die, the nation begins a religious and political downturn into both idolatry and anarchy. Throughout this period, a time covered in the Bible's book of Judges, the nation is periodically relieved from oppression by men and women whom God ordains and empowers. They are called Judges but the repetitive theme of the book of Judges is that there was no "King" in Israel and everyone did what was "right" in their own eyes. This period of Israel's history clearly displayed the fallacy of allowing "good" to be defined by individuals who do not recognize the ultimate authority of God or the objective and absolute definition of "goodness" which is his character and attributes.

Throughout the period during which Israel is occasionally rescued by individual "Judges" it also becomes clear that these men and women themselves remain subject to human error. It is also during this time that the priesthood of Israel is becoming increasingly corrupt. An aging priest named Eli, along with his sons, is replaced through the direct intervention of God with a young man named Samuel. The youthful Samuel grew up under Eli's tutelage and served Eli in the Tabernacle (an early form of what would eventually become the Temple).

For the first time in Israel's history a singular individual, Samuel, fills the role of priest while also introducing a new divinely appointed office – prophet. As prophet and priest, Samuel administers God's law while also enforcing its judgments through pronouncements that God fulfills. His rule over the nation is not universal however. Pockets of rebellion to God's law are evidenced by an ever increasing penetration of alternate theologies. As the nation continues to grow the tribal leaders, sometimes in conflict with one another, finally ask Samuel to give them a king. They do so in an effort to unite the nation under one head and to become like other nations with whom they periodically battle.

Distressed and clearly depressed by the request Samuel is nonetheless instructed by God to give the people what they "want." God instructs Samuel to tell the people that what they want is not what they need and that they will eventually come to regret that they wanted a human king, drawn from among them, rather than the Messiah God promised. The Messiah would not only deliver the nation from sinful nations around them but from sin and its curse.

The Bible books of I & II Samuel, I &II Kings as well I & II Chronicles contain the combined history, at times, duplicating stories, of Israel's experiment with a monarchy. The first king, Saul, is selected and anointed king by Samuel. His reign commences with an unusual occurrence. As King, Saul also begins to prophesy. At this unique period in Israel's history they have one man, Samuel, who is a priest and a prophet. At the same time, their king is also considered among the prophets. However it is Saul's attempt to unify all three offices, prophet, priest and king in himself to which God intervenes again and declares that Saul's reign will be cut short, that his heir will not sit on the throne of Israel and commands Samuel to go to the obscure village of Bethlehem to find another man to anoint as king of Israel. It is in this story that God's design for humanity is clarified. His design is for his Messiah alone (a being that will be both God and man) to fill all three offices of Prophet, Priest and King.

David, a shepherd and the youngest son of his father, Jesse, becomes the greatest king in Israel's history. The nation becomes completely united under his reign, enemies are largely vanquished and the treasury of Israel grows to the point where David's son, Solomon, is able to build both a palace for himself and the famous Temple of Solomon. Solomon's attention to God, however, is diluted by a truly outrageous number of wives (some gained through political alliances) and concubines. The Bible states that Solomon's wives turned his heart away from God and the nation suffered through another round of idolatrous intrusion into their theology.

Upon the death of Solomon, Israel's allegiance becomes divided between the north and south. Different kings rule in each for the remainder of Israel's monarchical period. Each and every king in the north is considered apostate by God and the northern kingdom is the first to be conquered and taken into captivity in Babylon (modern day Iraq). Although the southern kingdom fares somewhat better having at least a few kings who "did what was right in the eyes of God," their captivity into Babylon was postponed but equally inevitable.

Throughout the monarchical period God called various prophets to alert Israel to its idolatry and the kings to their obligations. The principal prophets during that time were Elijah and his protégé, Elisha. These men would periodically call Israel's attention to their idolatry; Elijah challenged the prophets of Baal to a contest wherein they were challenged to call fire down from heaven. After days of attempting to do so, the prophets of Baal gave up and turned the challenge over to Elijah. Elijah instructed that thousands of gallons of water be poured over the sacrificial altar he had prepared (something that would clearly make a fire originating from the ground impossible).

When Elijah prayed to God, he answered with fire from heaven that consumed the sacrifice and all of the water. In response, the prophets of Baal were immediately killed but that act enraged the king and his wife, Jezebel, and they attempted to kill God's prophets in kind.

It is during Israel's captivity in Babylon that God's prophets become the central voice of God's promised redemption. The Bible's books of prophecy are unusual literature. While the prophecies address immediate concerns they also forecasts future events beyond the scope of the issues at hand. The prophecies of three men in particular, Daniel, Isaiah and Ezekiel, point to a future time when God brings deliverance not just to Israel but through Israel to all nations.

The New Testament opens with four books called "The Gospels." Each presents historical events surrounding the life of Jesus including his teachings and conversations with a wide range of people. Three of the Gospels, Matthew, Mark and Luke, are called "synoptic" Gospels because they present accounts of the same or similar events but with unique perspectives and writing styles that seem to indicate the accounts were written to different audiences. The fourth Gospel, John, is significantly different from the other three. John's Gospel certainly includes his eyewitness accounts of events but his aim is considered much more interpretative in presenting a strong case that Jesus is truly the Son of God.

Christianity, as a separate theology, has its roots firmly entrenched in Judaism and the Hebrew nation's long awaited fulfillment of God's promise to provide a Messiah. At his appearance Messiah would fill all three of God's divinely ordained leadership roles, the offices of Prophet, Priest and King, and fulfill God's promise to provide a final atonement for all of humanity's sins. Prophecies concerning Messiah began in the Garden of Eden when God spoke directly to Eve explaining that she, and all women in the future would forever have difficulty in childbirth (pain and suffering) but that, one day, God would provide a singularly important offspring who would suffer a "bruised heel" from the act of crushing "the serpent." The prophecies continued throughout the history of Israel up and through the final prophecies recorded during the nation's captivity in Babylon. While too numerous to catalogue a few of the prophecies need to be understood in order to know why some, though not all, Jews came to believe that Jesus was the promised Messiah.

Old Testament prophecies specifically point out that Messiah would be in the lineage of Israel's greatest king, David. Messiah's lineage would, having gone through David, connect back through Abraham and, ultimately, to Adam and Eve. Messiah would be sinless at birth by virtue of being born of a virgin through the agency of God's Holy Spirit; He would be counted among thieves, hated and rejected by the nation of Israel.

Messianic prophecy painted a picture that ultimately confused Jews who lived through and witnessed the life of Jesus. On the one hand there were prophecies that clearly revealed a Messiah who would suffer on behalf of the nation. On the other there were those that illustrated his triumph over evil and the establishment of a permanent Kingdom where all of Israel would find peace and security under a King who would be their eternal Prophet and Priest as well. Up to the point of Jesus' birth the Jews did not consider the possibility that Messiah would actually suffer death. Nor did they understand that the prophecies might be divisible into two separate appearances or "comings" of Messiah.

The controversial nature of Jesus' teachings and their expectation of a King that would overthrow the Romans (who had conquered and occupied Israel) led the Jewish leadership and many ordinary Jews to miss the first appearance of their Messiah in the man, Jesus. His death was the result of an overwhelming rejection of his claim to be the Son of God. The message that Jesus delivered is recorded in the Gospels. It was certainly controversial. He told his followers on several occasions that he would be put to death but would also be resurrected. This completely confounded his own followers and, of course, the priests and lawyers that governed the Jews under the oversight of the Roman government. A large segment of Jewish leaders, called the Sadducees, did not even believe in the resurrection of human life let alone that of the promised Messiah.

The Gospels not only lay out this storyline in great detail but helped those who were able to read or hear the story after his resurrection understand that Jesus would return to fulfill the promise of Messiah's ultimate rule over the entire earth. The Gospels interpret the meaning of Jesus' life and death in addition to covering the historical events that led to his execution on a cross. The actual teachings of Jesus must be read to appreciate. It's not particularly difficult to read all of them in a single sitting either. Many New Testament printings show his actual words in red ink as opposed to black. Those who are unfamiliar with the teachings of Jesus should take the time to read those statements if nothing else.

A central theme in Jesus' teaching was to clarify the role of the Law in the lives of God's people. Like many "religions" Judaism had become more readily identified with what people did as opposed to what they really believed and who they were in relationship to God. Adhering to the letter of the Law did not, according to Jesus, bring salvation or provide for the full redemption of humanity from the curse of sin. The Law had, over time, served mostly to separate people into those who were "righteous" through ceremonial activity from those who failed in the smallest point of the Law. Jesus was routinely tested by a group of Jewish Law experts, called

Pharisees, who took great personal pride in their strict adherence to the Mosaic Law and the incidental laws developed over the history of Judaism to make that adherence complete. Jesus once pointed out to these lawyers that the Law was made to serve humanity not so that humanity should serve the Law.

Jesus was not a legalist in the sense that legalism is evident among certain Christian denominations today. His message was that no one is truly righteous except God. He taught that the gap of righteousness between God and humanity was so wide that it could only be bridged by a sovereign act of God and that God would bridge that gap through his death and resurrection.

The Gospels are followed by a fifth book called the "Acts of the Apostles" or just "Acts." This book, written by Luke (the author of the Gospel of Luke) continued to record the early history of Jesus' disciples after his resurrection and return to heaven. It is an important transitional book in that it establishes the mission to promote and preach the Gospel beyond the borders of Judaism. In this book, the emerging leadership of that mission is defined and those who were Jesus' closest followers begin to suffer great persecution and some are martyred.

One particularly zealous persecutor of Christians, a Jew and a Pharisee (lawyer) named Saul, has an encounter with the risen Christ through a blinding light from which Jesus speaks to him. He is humbled by the authority with which Jesus speaks to him and suffers temporary blindness. Instructed to proceed to a Christian disciple's home, Saul is ultimately healed from his blindness and begins a new mission (under a new name, Paul) to promote and expertly explain the teachings of Christ to Jews and Gentiles (a Gentile is anyone that is not Jewish) alike.

The book of Acts goes on to recount the life of Paul and three missionary journeys during which he ultimately turns his attention to Gentiles but without complete disregard of his fellow Jews. During his lifetime Paul writes letters to various churches in cities he has visited and/or churches he has helped establish. These letters, also called epistles, were routinely circulated among all the churches and become a significant portion of the New Testament.

Paul is the primary theologian of the Christian faith. The New Testament includes other epistles written by the Apostles John, Peter, James and Jude. Together, all of these epistles interpret the teachings of Jesus and their relationship to Judaism. They promote the extension of Judaism's foundation upon which Messiah's (Jesus') message and mission rests. They also clearly build upon that foundation a familiar theology wherein humanity's sinful nature is covered by the more powerful expression of God's grace through the atoning blood Jesus shed on the cross.

The epistles do not teach that humanity's sinful nature has been eliminated but provides an escape from the consequences of sin (which is an eternal death penalty) through an individual placing faith in the effectiveness of Jesus' atonement for sins when he died for all sins (past, present and future) on the cross. The epistles teach that placing one's faith in the atonement means acknowledging that Jesus is the Son of God and therefore the only possible innocent human worthy of shedding truly innocent blood as a substitutional sacrifice for the all of humanity's sins.

Furthermore, the resurrection of Jesus' body through the power of God's Holy Spirit that resided in him is the basis for which believers in Jesus will (through the same resident Holy Spirit in their bodies) one day rise from death to a life that is eternal and sinless. This sinless and eternal existence is the means through which humanity's communion with God is re-established so that in the eternal existence humanity will return to the same fellowship Adam and Eve enjoyed with God in the Garden of Eden.

The final book in the New Testament is a book called The Revelation. Its full title is "The Revelation of Jesus Christ to the Apostle John." It is the final book of prophecy in the Bible and describes the events leading up to the end of time. It was written by the Apostle John while he was being held in captivity on the Isle of Patmos. The literary style of the book combines two forms of prophecy. One style is generally called "forth-telling" because it speaks of conditions in the present (the "present" during John's time) and provides instructions and judgments for that time. The other style of prophecy is "foretelling." This is prophecy that gives humanity a glimpse of those things which are yet to happen in the future.

John points this out by stating that he is under instructions to show those things which were, those things which are, and those things which are yet to come. John's writing includes visions which are allegorically interpreted by the angel who is guiding his journey into the future. Aspects of the future are uniquely similar to prophecies contained in the Old Testament books of Daniel, Isaiah and Ezekiel.

Although Christian theologians differ on aspects of timing most agree that the prophecy shows the imminent return of Jesus to the earth where he will fulfill those portions of prophecy from the Old Testament where Messiah rules and reigns over an earthly Kingdom. The prophecy foretells of the resurrection of all humanity to face judgment before the "White Throne" of God. All who have failed to acknowledge Jesus as the Son of God and therefore rejected his atoning sacrifice will be cast into a lake of fire (hell) for all of eternity. Those who have placed their faith in Jesus and his atonement will go onto everlasting life in heaven equipped with new, glorified bodies, which are incapable of sin and death.

## PART FIVE

## THEOLOGICALLY APPLIED ECONOMICS
*Can there be heaven on earth?*

By this time you no doubt already know the answer. It is a resounding "NO." But, in fairness to the unconvinced it is only appropriate to build up to that answer using what has been presented thus far. It has been established that humanity is unique in all of creation in that we possess the freedom and capacity to believe whatever it is that pleases us individually. We have the capacity to make a judgment on the relative benefits of placing faith in either humanity individually (literally in one's self) or in something or someone beyond which nothing greater can be conceived.

This judgment, a decision ultimately, is so primary that it precedes any other possible decision. It literally forms the foundation upon which all other decisions are made. It is the only means of determining whether any action is "good" or "bad." The sensory limitations of humanity coupled with its unique capacity to know those limitations forces all individual humans to justify their behavior whenever they encounter another human possessing, as all humans do, the same freedom to act.

Whenever individuals choose to place their faith in their own sovereignty, social groups of humans will struggle to reconcile all those varying concepts of what is ultimately "good" or "bad" for the society. Even though many individuals could agree on broad concepts of what is "good," the social organization will always be governed by force. At times a majority of opinion will win the day; it is just as likely historically that it could be accomplished through force of power. In either case it will pit one ideology against that of others. Since social groups coalesce around those things commonly believed to be "good," that choice will, by definition, categorize alternate ideas as "bad."

Without a universally accepted set of "good" actions that kind of society will never be able to operate an economy that requires everyone to be "good." Communism, for example, will fail because it presumes that individuals can be made to act in ways beneficial to others in society. This presumption is without historic precedent. Individuals will *sometimes* act in ways that are beneficial to others – even at their own expense. But communism can only work if that kind of behavior is perpetual and sustainable. Of course it can't be since that which is determined by others to be good for most people will, by definition, be "bad" for others.

History has shown that individuals operating in self-faith will eventually circumvent any restriction that promotes a "bad" result for them as individuals. Communism doesn't fail because of bad *intentions* it fails because of *unavoidable contentions* between individuals. Likewise, the more moderate forms of communism, like socialism, do not take the flawed nature of humanity into account. In the case of socialism the degree to which capital is seized from productive individuals for redistribution to less productive individuals will progressively diminish the incentive to produce.

Christian theology begins with the assumption that God exists, that he is the Sovereign of the universe, stands outside of the entire creation, including time, and is independent of its inherent limitations. It holds that mankind is part of God's creation and that humanity's position is unique in that mankind represents the only creature made in God's image. While the depth and richness of God's character and attributes are beyond our capacity to fully comprehend, God provided through his Word (Scripture) a revelation of all that is necessary for humanity to know what is dependably "good." We also know that we have been given the freedom to accept or reject this "goodness," or to continue developing our own sense of what is right in competition with everyone else.

For Christians, mankind's persistence in electing to reject God is simply more evidence of humanity's flawed nature. But Christians also acknowledge that even our choice to accept God's Sovereignty in the universe does not make *us* "good" and certainly not *"better"* than anyone else. Christians acknowledge that all of humanity is flawed by a powerful delusion that we are the measure of all things and that our decisions do not need to stand the test of the absolute right and wrong God provides in his Word. While humanity appears very comfortable living in shades of gray it is those shades between black and white that causes wars.

When expressed in economic policy, it means that human beings will naturally attempt to build capital in quantities sufficient to realize their own personal dreams. Although all individuals will believe that their personal ambitions and dreams are good, history has shown that humans will do almost anything to realize those dreams even if it is at the expense of others. However a reasonably restricted capitalistic economy will force even bad endeavors (selfishness and greed, etc.) into compliance so that only successful goods and services *ultimately* succeed. Success is determined by customer satisfaction and competition drives producers to continually increase satisfaction through innovation.

It is an unavoidable reality that capitalism also allows failures to occur. Failures are expensive to society and produce significant pain to those individuals who fail. Socialistic policies that seek to ease the pain of individual failure or provide essential goods and services to those who are unable to produce capital on their own are admittedly filled with good intentions. A Christian theology, however, doesn't automatically place the burden of distributing relief on the government. In fact, it is the duty of the *church*. When the church distributes relief the recipient becomes even more aware that God is the only source of goodness and that his blessings provide the depository from which the poor and oppressed find comfort.

There are practical considerations for turning benevolence back to the churches of America. One is that the Government's methodology of dispensing benevolence fosters a permanent poverty class. This happens because those who receive Government assistance do so in relative privacy. Checks come in the mail or are now electronically dispersed directly into the recipient's checking account. Since there is no personal connection to the disbursement of benevolence there is no way of knowing whether the assistance is becoming addictive or not.

Benevolence that is administrated by churches is provided on an as needed when needed basis. People have to come to the church in order to get those things or funds they need understanding that what they're receiving is a gift, not a right. As such they are much more attuned to the costs their benevolence has on those from whom they obtain sustenance. They are forced to socialize with the very people who are providing for them and that alone provides a powerful incentive for the giver and receiver to find productive work for the recipient. It doesn't even have to be explained that churches will administrate benevolence far more efficiently than government can or ever will.

For Christians, the most vexing economic consideration is just how "restricted" capitalism should be. The question arises from the realization that, given humanity's flawed nature, there will be elements of the economy that are inordinately subject to personal manipulation. It is possible in a capitalistic economy for concentrations of capital to unduly empower individuals or small groups of individuals such that a significant competitive advantage will produce monopolies. In fact, history has shown that without some form of regulation monopolies will form and will, in turn, hamper the real engines of capital formation – small businesses.

When inequities in the economy are discovered humans tend to form alliances to fight against those whose power hampers or eliminates their access to capital. In the case of monopolies and powerful employers those alliances have historically been among the laborers. Trade Unions can only succeed, however, in economic environments where other sources of labor are difficult to obtain.

The strength of collective bargaining has historically been too easy to circumvent. In American history this resulted in violence, riots and economic disturbance. When alliances, like unions, aren't enough, humans will form (and then look to) governments to enforce the free flow of capital and equal opportunity. It is very important here to once again note that history has proven that governments emerge from *economic* responses by individuals who have built economic alliances among themselves first before even considering competing structures of government.

Christian theology supports the formation of governments (the types are covered in the next section) that are invested with the responsibility to ensure the free flow of capital and equal opportunity. Christian theology supports a reasonable level of economic regulation as well. The question is really not whether economic regulation is necessary but how much?

Christians believe that God is Sovereign and proactively intervenes in the affairs of humanity. The regulation of the economy should not interfere with God's will for individuals and families because government intervention thwarts the underlying dependence humanity *should* have on God. How can that magical balance of intervention be determined? The test has to be simple and understandable or else it will never be practical.

It *is* simple. If a government seeks to intervene into the economic affairs of individuals the question should be asked, "If enacted, will this regulation tip the dependency of the individual to the side of government dependency or help the individual continue to depend on God?" If it tips toward government Christians should not support it.

In America's political parlance this is often referred to as "rugged individualism." Rugged individualism may be a great sounding adjective but it is not the reason individuals really succeed. This is not to deny that individuals have talents that are greater than those of others. Talent certainly goes a long way toward making an individual succeed. It also does not deny that individuals need resources to invest in their work. But it is proper Christian theology to acknowledge that God, by his sovereign will, blesses everyone with those talents and will provide resources from his treasury to help anyone succeed. The term, "rugged individualism," should be replaced in Christian vocabulary with "humble dependence."

Through humble dependence Christians actively submit to the plans and will of God. To illustrate this point Jesus once encouraged his disciples to pray and ask God openly for the things they wanted and needed. He told them that if a child asks a father for a piece of bread the father would not give the child a stone. "If," he said, "you being human would not give your child a stone, how much more will your Father in heaven give you the things for which you ask?"

For Christians it is no shame to be "dependent" if that dependency is on God. It is, in fact, our joy. When it comes to economics our policies should be much more unified than they are because the teaching of God's Word could not be clearer. There will never be a heaven on earth as long as our Messiah delays his return. In the interim period, we need to support those economic policies that grow society's dependence on God while not allowing ourselves to become dependent on a very poor substitute – government.

Christian theology also acknowledges the harsh realities of life and one of those is that ours may never be more than a minority view. Economic dependence upon God is just one of several beliefs that subject Christians to ridicule in societies where our theology is not widely embraced. Given the flawed nature of humanity, mankind's drive toward self validation is very strong. The root of humanity's "flaw" is, after all, the propensity to reject the idea of a Supreme Being in favor of self determination. This is the very basis upon which Maslow developed his "hierarchy of needs." The highest need, according to Maslow, is "self-actualization."

Those who live outside of Christianity's theology find the idea of depending on God counterintuitive. It just doesn't make sense and it makes even less sense to them when they see or hear of Christians expressing their dependence on God for even the smallest of things. The idea of actually choosing a lifestyle that is inherently humiliating to one's sense of self just does not *look* attractive. This is one reason Jesus told his followers that the path to heaven would be narrow and its gate would be small compared to the wide path and huge gate leading into hell. The original temptation in the Garden says it all. Eve was told she would become like God when she disobeyed him and ate from the forbidden tree. The most difficult thing for any human being is to surrender one's ego.

It is also sad to say that Christianity suffers from a "black eye" whenever some misguided preacher claims that Christian theology promises wealth from God's hand. The idea that Christians are more important to God than anyone else and that God's blessings will guarantee abundance to all who simply believe in him is ridiculous. It doesn't take a great deal of intellect to shoot this one down. Whenever a Christian comes to believe that God is an automatic dispensary of wealth to those who are "good," it clearly moves that believer away from acknowledging God's Sovereignty. We must remember – it is his will that is to be done and not our own. When Scripture says that the rains fall on the good as well as the bad it means that God provides for all of humanity whether they recognize him or not. It also means that those who are supposedly "good" will have no more rain than anyone else.

Since Christians themselves are not any "better" than anyone else when it comes to humanity's flawed condition ridicule isn't coming from only those outside the faith but, as evidenced in the preceding paragraph, inside as well. Within the community of Christianity, theology has not been uniformly settled. The interpretation of Scripture given here is certainly not universally accepted among all of Christianity's adherents. To varying degrees individual Christians struggle to keep their own ego in check. Groups of Christians that gather into churches sometimes take a great deal of pride in what they achieve be that recognition, wealth, influence in the community or, usually, their success as compared to other churches.

The question then becomes rather straight forward; is Christian theology practical? If its practice flies in the face of reality – the fact that humanity is flawed and will not (even within a community of Christians) ever accept the diminished role of "creature," shouldn't economic freedom be highly restricted to virtually guarantee that all of humanity enjoys an equal result from life?

The biggest flaw in that argument is the presumption that humanity actually *wants* equal results among themselves. They don't. Instead, individual humans struggle mightily to establish a unique identity. Nothing will be more frustrating to humanity than waking each morning to discover that they are merely average. If the economy is highly restricted and government enlarged to the point where humans depend on its efficient function to ensure that everyone gets the same results out of life humanity will see that those "equal" results will always sink to the lowest standard of equality rather than to its highest potential. Those who do not produce enough to meet the average level will continuously drag the rest of humanity down.

Capitalism is the only economic model that starts by acknowledging the true nature of humanity. Even so, it has its challenges. It provides absolutely no guarantee individuals will succeed. In fact, without reasonable restrictions it can and does produce dangerous inequities. Whenever equal opportunity's fire is extinguished by the lack of capital's oxygen, some form of intervention is required. That intervention, however, should have one goal and one goal only – to make capital accessible for production rather than capital for mere sustenance.

Capital that is accumulated by the wealthy is only useful when it is redeployed through investments in human ingenuity and productivity. Reasonable restrictions on capitalism should eliminate monopolies and foster competition among humans. Direct investments through the private sector of the economy are clearly more efficient that running capital through the government for distribution. For one thing, governments are inherently inefficient when their only purpose is to take money from the left hand and move it to the right hand. It is also an unavoidable reality that whenever government decides to take capital away from anyone for the purposes of distributing it to someone else the decision of who receives the "distribution" will become a calculation of who benefits the lawmaker the most from a political standpoint.

The basic idea that accumulated capital should generally be put back to use through investments directed by the private sector of the economy is often called "supply-side" economics. During the 1980's its detractors called it "trickle-down" economics and painted a visual representation of the wealthy as fat and self-absorbed people whose pockets were so filled with money that an occasional dollar or two would slip out and trickle down to the less fortunate who were left waiting for crumbs from the largess of the inattentive rich.

It was proposed, instead, that government needed to squeeze the pockets of the wealthy so that more dollars could be captured by the government and forcibly directed specifically to those people in need. The idea was visually compelling and called "trickle-up" economics. It was thought that money dispersed by the government would be spent by those in need and would fuel the economy toward expansion and growth. The idea that capital would only "trickle" up to the rich sounded much better to most people because most people weren't (and still aren't) rich.

The underlying assumption was that government could "produce" jobs and opportunity by redistributing capital. In the language of politics the government not only speaks of producing jobs but specifically attributes job creation to the President and Congress. It may be disappointing to presidential and congressional campaign managers but the fact is government simply does not "produce" anything. It can't unless, of course, it takes over segments of the economy through what is called nationalizing.

Nationalizing an industry or groups of industries is done by many countries throughout the world. It generally begins by a government taking over critical industries tied to either national security or services that must be available to all citizens regardless of their ability to pay for it. Airlines are commonly nationalized as is the production of oil in the Arab states and Venezuela. The most familiar service that is commonly nationalized is the postal service. The latest nationalization in America has been the government takeover of two of the three largest automobile manufacturers – General Motors and Chrysler. These were taken over by the government on the assumption that they were too large and important to fail. The truth was each manufacturer had too many employees (voters) to ignore.

Although a nationalized postal service was clearly appropriate when the nation was founded, private competition today has nearly made the U.S. postal service obsolete. The Postal Service's inability to effectively compete with the private sector has led to an ever increasing cost of postage and, most recently, the closure of post offices around the country and the reduction of the work week from six days to five. Government may be able to take over industries through legislation and thereby claim to be "producing" something but history has shown that the government is an inefficient manager of those industries when compared to the private sector.

Imagine a huge circle that represents the total consumption (not production) of goods within the United States' economy. Within that circle (a classic pie chart) segments are marked representing that portion which represents the private sector's consumption and that of the nation's government. Now imagine a modestly larger circle, representing everything produced in America is drawn to encompass the circle of consumption. It is always hoped that America will continue to produce more than it consumes so that the inner circle that represents private and government consumption never expands beyond the country's production capacity.

Government consumption is always at the expense of private consumption. The government actually competes for the same productive capacity and "capital" from which Americans hope to find resources that will fuel their lives and work. In the United States the government has three ways to obtain the capital required to support its consumption. It can tax those who produce capital which includes individuals and companies. It can borrow funds, which temporarily takes those funds out of productive use and forces the private sector to pay more in interest for the capital it borrows. Or, it can simply print more money.

If the government borrows money it must eventually be repaid. While it is unpaid it is added to the "national debt." In order to eventually pay its debts the government has to hope that the economy will produce enough so that future taxes on the private sector can repay the debt or, at the very least, continue to pay the interest on the debt.

Whenever a government prints more money in order to fund its own consumption the currency of the country is devalued. That simply means that since there are more dollars in the system each individual dollar is worth a little less than it was before the government printed more. Economists call this inflation because the total amount of capital in the system is inflated whenever the government elects to print more money.

For example assume the government wanted to purchase 2,000 fighter jets but did not have the $20 billion costs in its budget; it could simply print $20 billion in fresh, new bills and pay the manufacturer for the jets. That money would then be paid out to subcontractors and parts manufacturers and would make its way into the economy.

Over a few weeks or perhaps even days there would suddenly be more dollars in the economy but those dollars would be available for the same number of goods that the economy had before the government printed more money. More money and fewer goods will make the price of everything go up and suddenly the money citizens have in their banks is worth less than it once was.

Whenever the government's appetite for capital grows its hunger must be satisfied at the expense of the capital fueling the private sector. As government consumption grows it crowds into and competes with the private sector. Its expansion can eventually cut off the private sector's access to critical capital forcing it into what's commonly called a recession. Recessions are defined as time when the productive output of the private sector drops for four straight months. This is why capital should remain in the private sector whenever possible. Government growth penalizes productivity in each and every instance. In fact it has been shown that tax cuts fuel growth so efficiently in the private sector that government ends up collecting more dollars than it would otherwise have collected without cutting taxes. It should be pointed out for clarity that this, of course, couldn't happen if taxes were eliminated entirely.

The argument in support of reasonably restricted capitalism is not new nor is it uniquely "Christian." However Christian theology supports it on the basis that it acknowledges humanity's flaw of self-indulgence while harnessing what is essentially greed so that selfishness is positively directed toward productivity.

Christians believe that they are only temporary citizens of the earth. They look forward to the fulfillment of God's plan to one day redeem them along with all of creation when Jesus returns to establish the Kingdom of God. Christians know that this Kingdom already exists but does so in a kind of exile outside of time. Christians believe that they are already citizens of that Kingdom. In fact, they have already entered into eternity but struggle to tolerate time's limitations over their physical existence. Christians know they remain subject to death and the inconvenience of aging but still rest in the hope that God does provide for their physical and emotional needs while they are trapped in time's grasp.

## THEOLOGICALLY APPLIED POLITICS
*Can't We All Just Get Along?*

If Christian theology supports one economic system over all others does it also support only one form of governance? This is a much more difficult question to answer because Scripture records enough history to show the results of nearly every form of human political organization. Monarchies, oligarchies, and various forms of democracies are seen as well as despotic forms of dictatorship. Just being included in the historical account, however, certainly doesn't mean that these forms were commended. In fact, nearly every form of government is shown to be ultimately difficult to sustain given mankind's proclivity to selfish individualism.

The Hebrew people were organized around a patriarchal system from the calling of Abraham up to and including the time of his grandson, Joseph. Joseph's untimely departure into Egypt served to acquaint him with a classical monarchical government led by Egypt's Pharaohs. The government of the Hebrew nation under the rule of Moses was predicated on a theocracy wherein God, through the pillar of fire by night and the cloud by day, actually led the people directionally. Moses met with God in the "tent of meeting" and took direction from God in providing a Law to the people. There were elements of representative organization in the execution of justice among the tribes but God, himself, also judged the people as was evidenced when a man, Achan, secretly hid a wedge of gold taken as booty from the fall of Jericho in his tent. God directed Joshua to use a type of lottery system to identify Achan as the culprit.

As Israel entered into its own monarchical period Scripture clearly points out the folly of God's people looking to a system to guarantee their safety and good fortune. Scripture is clear that no form of government is as reliable as the theocracy that is promised at the end of time. However, one clue as to how Christians "ought" to govern themselves is provided in the organization of the church as described in the New Testament. The difficulty is that this form of organization was never expressly taught by the Apostles to be projected onto the civilization of humanity as a whole.

Church government is called polity. The early church's government was not unlike the kind of government exercised by the Jewish leaders of the synagogue. That should not be a great surprise since most adherents of early Christianity were Jews. Churches were first established by apostolic leadership meaning that one of the twelve original Apostles generally founded the local church. The practice after founding was to establish a group of elders led by one elder who acted as "bishop" of the church. These leaders in turn selected or caused elections to be held to choose deacons who were charged with the administration of the church's funds and benevolence activities.

As the original Apostles died their respective protégé's and the bishops governing the church in each city emerged as the next leadership with the authority to validate theological belief and religious practice. Although disagreements among the bishops were rare in the first three centuries of the new theology, conflicts over how to handle various heresies eventually led to the emergence of the bishop at Rome holding a position of authority over all other bishops. The bishop of Rome's preeminence, however, wasn't really established until the fifth and sixth Centuries during the papacies of Leo and Gregory the Great respectively. In both cases the breakdown of the Roman government led both to fill the gap. However it can be graciously concluded, with all due respect to the Catholic tradition of Christianity, that the papacy itself (the preeminence of a human patriarch) fostered as much corruption as quality leadership. As stated before, Christianity does not hold the theological view that simply being "Christian" changes the basic flawed nature of men or women.

The traditions of Christianity and human history point to the conclusion that, absent an expressed Scriptural basis for human government, the best approach is to establish a government system that at least takes into account the fallen nature of humanity. What has already been explored in terms of economic behavior is useful in selecting that form of government that best serves humanity. Economic history has demonstrated the effectiveness of capitalism. It has the ability to harness the conflicting wills of individuals by forcing an individual's desires to be profitable. Profitable, in the case, means gaining the support of enough other individuals to sustain a livelihood.

Democracy in its purest form operates under the assumption that a simple majority of individuals, each with the power to vote, establishes law and policy. In small manageable groups this "one person

– one vote" system works well. However, as societal populations grow that system can break down when problems have more than a few solutions. It is possible in a pure democracy that a single solution will not gain the support of a simple majority.

For example, suppose a town of 300 individuals operates a copper mine that is equally owned by all residents. Having reached the end of a particularly prosperous vein the town must decide on a direction for a new tunnel in the mine. The options include going north, south, east or west. While the most knowledgeable miners in the town favor going north and are able, through their expertise, to convince a large number of residents, they are not able to get 151 people to vote with them. They may have more votes than any other group but, without a majority in favor of their advice, a larger group will oppose their plan – even if that larger group has less agreement between them.

Pure democracy, then, can be stultifying. Throughout history larger governments have relied on representative forms of democracy. Representative forms allow a "plurality" of opinion to decide policy and frequently, through advanced lobbying skills, achieve majorities that might otherwise be impossible. Representatives form alliances of convenience that enable them to win concessions that are important to their constituents while trading concessions to other representatives when those concessions do not materially harm their own constituents. This kind of "horse-trading" has been a hallmark of the House of Representatives and the British House of Commons.

But, abuses of power led representative democracies to use a system of checks and balances which moderated those policies enacted by a plurality rather than a clear majority. This has been done mostly by introducing a "bi-cameral" form of representation where two separate representative bodies are tasked to evaluate the same policy. The second body has generally consisted of a group that is given greater latitude by making it less answerable to the immediate public. In some cases, the second group has been made up of nobles who inherit their position. In America, that group is called the Senate and the Senate is insulated from the mood swings of the public by making their term of service longer than that of the House of Representatives. This length of service (6 years) allows Senators the opportunity to serve three times the length of House members. Through this length of service, Senators are less subject to the immediate whims of the public and even the President whose term is four years.

At its founding, America also included a system whereby the President has to sign legislation in order for it to become law but, through a check and balance measure in the Constitution, gave both representative houses the opportunity to override a Presidential veto by making laws that have two-thirds support in both representative bodies. America also instituted an independent judiciary that interprets the laws' conformity to the Constitution.

Christian theology cannot be said to support only this form of government but can, because of its checks and balances and representative form, acknowledge its inherent strength to accomplish politically what capitalism accomplishes economically. American Christians can and do support America's form of government regardless of their own individual religious practice or denominational affiliation.

One final note is important to include in this discussion. Christian theology expressly (in Romans 13) forbids Christians from participating in rebellion against the powers of the government. This portion of Scripture identifies all those in power as individuals whom God has placed there. The inference is that as the Universal Sovereign, God's will, in terms of "who" is at the helm of government, will be done in spite of humanity's individual freedom of choice.

This is particularly hard for American Christians to grasp. For one thing, it means that our founding fathers' rebellion against King George was not in conformity with Scripture. However, it also means that the success of the rebellion was ordained by God. Given the precedent set by the American colonial rebellion, some Christians feel that future rebellions should be justifiable. While the Declaration of Independence sets out the rational terms for a rebellion it is not Scripture.

The main reason Christianity teaches against rebellion is that it circumvents the faith Christians must place in that beyond which nothing greater can be conceived. God, by virtue of his being, is the Sovereign of the Universe and his Word (Scripture) clearly shows that it is he and no other that governs the leadership of the world. Rebellion against the government is said (in Romans 13) to actually be rebellion against God. What then is a Christian to do when a government becomes oppressive? There has never been a greater oppression in history than that which the early Christian Church endured at the hands of the Roman Empire. The writing of Romans chapter 13 was concluded during that persecution and the writer, himself, was martyred in that persecution.

As Americans, whether theologically Christian or not, we are all blessed with the power to vote for or against our representatives and even to submit legislation through the processes of petition and referendum. Christians have enjoyed the pleasure of having many American representatives share their faith and theology. It has, however, become increasingly clear that most Christians (and some of those who represent Americans in government) do not believe their theology should take precedence over political ideology. In terms of Christian theology that position is not internally consistent with Scripture – it is not Christian theology at all but is certainly more "politically palatable" or, in modern thought, more "politically correct."

Christian theology forms the foundation upon which all other social policy should be based – and Christians should be unified in that theology. That means that since economic and political policy is subordinate to theology, Christians should be far more united than they are in terms of those policies. Christian theology expressly admits that all of humanity has the right to freely choose to accept or reject its theology but does not support the surrender of its principles in the interest of getting along with others.

Christians are not obliged to support alternate theologies or their expression in policy. That being said, they are clearly obliged to live under the laws established by their governments even when those governments are based on theologies in conflict with it. While remaining obedient to duly authorized laws, Christians should be economically and politically active in lobbying for policies consistent with Christian theology. However all Christians need to be assured that, in accordance with our theology, we can depend upon God to achieve his will in the universe and also depend on the life he has promised us when time, as we understand it, comes to an end. Christians are citizens of an eternal Kingdom first, citizens of earth and its various governments second. While living in the grasp of time Christians should exercise their rights as citizens to positively affect economic and political policy toward a theology that is consistent with Christianity.

# POLITICAL PARTIES

America's two-party political system has dominated its history even though there has been, from time to time, significant third parties influencing elections. The emergence of two parties began almost immediately after the nation's founding even though it was discouraged by George Washington. While the opinion of Americans within individual parties has often flip-flopped and the parties have, at times, exchanged constituencies one thing has been consistent: there have always been at least two sides to every issue and, strangely, Christians have vigorously aligned themselves on both sides.

At various times throughout America's history one or another political party has enjoyed wider support among Christians than the other. At present, a survey conducted the Barna Research Group, the research division of The Barna Group, Ltd. (a private, non-partisan, for profit organization), sheds light on the breakdown of American adults between the political descriptions "liberal" and "conservative." The study is published on its internet site (http://www.barna.org) with a date of March 27, 2009 and provides commentary on research conducted between August and November of 2008.

The commentary on the results is quoted here:

Based upon an evaluation of more than a dozen religious beliefs of liberals and conservatives, consistent and significant differences are evident. Liberals are less than half as likely as conservatives to firmly believe that the Bible is totally accurate in all of the principles it teaches (27% versus 63%, respectively); to strongly believe that Satan is real (17% versus

36%); and to firmly contend that they have a personal responsibility to share their religious beliefs with others (23% versus 48%)...

Liberals are also much less likely than conservatives to believe that "God is the all-knowing, all-powerful creator of the world who still rules the universe today." Only about half of liberals (55%) adopt that view of God compared to more than four out of five conservatives (82%)...

The research also revealed that liberals are twice as likely as conservatives to be categorized as "unchurched" (40% vs. 19%, respectively), while conservatives were twice as likely as liberals to be categorized as having an "active faith" (45% vs. 21%, respectively, defined as having read the Bible, attended a religious service <u>and</u> prayed to God during the past week).

This survey has important ramifications for Christians who want to become more in tune with Christian theology but also more politically active. It is very important that Christians try to accept realities (as they exist in our situation right now) without passing unnecessary judgments on individuals who align with either "liberal" or "conservative" parties. It would be more theologically consistent for Christians to remember that purity of belief in the most fundamental precepts of Christian theology is more important than one's political affiliation even when that affiliation puts the individual Christian into a group less likely to agree with their theology.

While the results of this survey suggest that liberals are less likely to identify with Christian theology than conservatives it has to be acknowledged that 55% of the liberals surveyed believe in the God Christian theology describes. Likewise it should be noted that even though 82% of conservatives hold that belief, those conservatives still associate with the 18% who don't. The greatest news from this survey is that an overwhelming majority of American adults believe that "God is the all-knowing, all-powerful creator of the world who still rules the universe today."

If that is true, and there is no reason to doubt the findings, it must also be true that American Christians are suffering from theological schizophrenia – an inability to translate their theology into an internally consistent economic and political personality. If they were, there would be much more alignment among Christians in their political affiliations.

The only explanation for the political alignment divergence among Christians is that they either do not have a consistent agreement on what their theology means or that they just won't translate that theology into economic and political policy because they fear it is politically incorrect to do so.

It would be easy to criticize that conclusion if one *assumed* that all of the foregoing discussion had as its aim to get all Christians aligned with one or the other political party. It is vitally important that Christians avoid that conclusion for one very good reason. Both major political parties in America are constantly in search of a majority to assure the longevity of their power. Humans, whether Christian or not, are prone to self-indulgence and the pursuit of personal gain. If anything at all has been historically proved in American history it is that neither political party has ever ensured the endurance of Christian theology in America.

Christians need to understand that American political parties need them more than they need the political party. If through education and honest dialogue American Christians can unite around those theological principles in which its eternal hope is based, nothing could stop it from having a majority-sized impact on the economic and social policies of America. If that kind of dream has any chance of realization it must be preceded by two things. First, American Christians simply must become more conversant and knowledgeable about their own belief structure. Secondly they must also continue to categorically act with graciousness toward the very large segment of Americans who do not hold the same theological views.

Christians must never lose sight of the fact that morally defensible laws will never convert a single non-believer. They must never become as arrogant as to believe that having passed morally defensible laws that they will thereby become "better" than any other members of humanity. All policy, whether economic or social, must have as its end the gracious administration of God's love to all of mankind. The story of God, as revealed in the Bible, is a story of redemption and all policies need to have the same redeeming quality. While abortion, for example, cannot be tolerated by Christian theology, any law forbidding it must be accompanied by social policy which provides the means to ensure that the life of the unborn is not destined to despair.

Likewise Christian theology would not support a political policy that in any way infringes those rights which are endowments of God like those already recognized in the Declaration of Independence. The Constitutional rights to a free press, free expression, free association, freedom from religious oppression and the freedom to exercise religion are rights consistent with those God granted humanity at

163

creation. Christian theology does not support a State run religion like those proposed and practiced in Islamic countries. As the writer of Hebrews in the New Testament pointed out, the Law does not bring salvation.

The message of this book is simple. Christians need to know what they believe and they need to begin building a consistently unified block of opinion and political activity based on that belief. They must remain independent enough to leverage their political and economic influence among all political parties. But, above all, Christians should heed these words spoken by Abraham Lincoln:

With Malice toward none, with charity for all, with firmness in the right, as God gives us to see the right, let us strive on to finish the work we are in, to bind up the nation's wounds.

***

## QUESTIONS & ANSWERS

**Would you share a little bit more about yourself?**

Sure. I was born and raised in Denver, Colorado and attended Evangel University, from 1975 to 1979, where I earned a Bachelor's of Business Administration Degree (B.B.A) with a major in business management and a concentration in social sciences. During my undergraduate years I served an internship with United States Senator, Jack Danforth, Republican, from Missouri. After graduation I spent 18 years in the chemical fertilizer industry. For 5 of those years I owned Affiliated Marketing Services, Inc., which I sold in 1995. In 2004 I began the process of earning a Master's in Theological Studies from the Assemblies of God Theological Seminary. I graduated with that degree in 2006. Throughout my life I have taught Bible courses in traditional Christian education environments and have, at times, written curricula for those courses.

**Let's begin with the title of your book. You titled it "Journey to Unity." Why a "journey?"**

Before I started writing I was contemplating my own journey in life. Throughout my life I have lived through the "curse" of constant evaluation. For better or worse I have never been able to escape the urge to take in information (in all forms) and reduce it down to its individual parts. Every part of information one considers can be taken as a proposition that demands proof and, if proven, moves one to then consider the decisions that proof requires. It's an intellectual and spiritual journey and, in my case, that trip has forced me to consider my life's events.

Those events have been the mirror into which I have frequently gazed. I have seen my own inconsistencies and I have also seen the results of attempting, at least, to live a principled life.

This book is a portrait of my journey from the most elemental foundation of my life through the steps that have taken me to the point of carefully evaluating where America, as a nation, stands in relationship to my deeply held beliefs. I don't believe that I am unique in the sense that my journey is like that of all humanity. My responses (my life decisions) have certainly taken me down a unique path but the journey itself is something that no one can completely avoid. I hope that the evaluation of my own journey serves some kind of higher purpose in perhaps helping others recognize the signs along the road. If those familiar signs are honestly considered I believe Americans can follow a path that leads to greater unity than is experienced now. So, my book is built with the tools of hope on a foundation of a faith that I think most people can claim as their own in their very own unique way.

## Do you really believe that Christians can form a new majority in America?

Christians already enjoy a majority position in the United States but do not fully capitalize on that strength. Christians are fragmented along religious and political lines and the only thing that can unify them is a return to biblical literacy. I'm confident that by returning to a biblically-based theology, American Christians can translate their shared beliefs into a more unified political policy that represents a majority within the United States.

**You write a lot about "biblical literacy;" what does that really mean?**

I realize that biblical literacy can be defined in several ways and that most Christians, no matter how it is defined, will feel the task is too daunting. Biblical literacy, however, does not require every Christian to become an "expert" theologian. At a minimum, however, Christians should return to the practice of reading the Bible on a daily basis. Daily reading inspires devotion and spiritual growth but the goal should also be to develop study habits that progressively build a knowledge base of principles from which theology is built.

**You make early references to the Judeo-Christian ethics yet you spend no substantial space addressing Jews. Why is that?**

From an ethical standpoint there should not be significant theological differences between Jews and Christians. It is important, however, to make a distinction here. The message of my book is directed specifically to Christians who, in various ways, identify themselves with the fundamental theological views of that faith. If I were to include a message to Jews who continue to retain a theological (rather than political or cultural) view consistent with Judaism I believe that group would find a great deal in common with Christian theology with the obvious acknowledgement that they do not believe that Jesus was their promised Messiah.

While Christian theology expressly incorporates Jewish Scripture and the theology of that Scripture, Judaism does not accept Christian theology as defined in the New Testament because they view

Jesus as an imposter. Still, Christian theology holds a very favorable view toward the Hebrew nation as God's chosen people and that view is manifested in a mutual interest in seeing Jerusalem become a uniformly Jewish city and the borders of Israel expanded to include their God-ordained inheritance. Christians believe that Jesus will physically return to Jerusalem a second time in the last days and that his return will result in the deliverance of the Jewish nation from their enemies forever.

The promise of the Messiah is shared by the two faiths but Christianity holds that Jesus fulfilled Old Testament Prophecy in part through his life and death nearly two millennia ago.

**In the Preface of your book, you write that 19th Century congregations were nearly as familiar with Scripture as their clergymen. That seems like an overstatement. Is it?**

I confess that like most writers I am occasionally prone to hyperbole. In this case, however, history bears out the fact that the Bible was the most read book (certainly the most widely published book) of that era. My comment is not intended to suggest that preachers in the 19th Century did not have considerably more knowledge of theology than the congregants. But it is safe to say that any significant departure, from essential Christian theological principle, would have been noticed by most of the congregations of those days.

**Do you think that modern Christian preachers are also theologians?**

Wow! That's a loaded question! Let me see; what would Jesus say? Let's break that question down a bit so that I don't end up making broad generalizations that will offend everyone. First, not all Christian preachers in America have received an education specifically in theology. Some don't even have a college or university degree in biblical studies. It's pretty safe to say, however, that among those preachers without formal undergraduate degrees in biblical studies most do not last without significant levels of consistent personal study, which, in some cases, provides a better education that the universities.

So far, I hope I haven't unduly offended anyone. I would point out, however, that there remains a significantly large segment of American Christians who really don't care if their preacher is a theologian. In too many cases, these Christians simply find their preacher too entertaining to swap out for someone who happens to be more learned. That is the major point I'm making in the Preface. American Christians today really don't possess the biblical literacy in sufficient numbers to keep entertainers out of their pulpits or build an expectation that sermons need to do more than simply entertain.

It is not enough to have a few elders or deacons in the local church monitor the theological consistency of preachers. Average, everyday congregants need to have enough study under their belt to spot the wolves masquerading as sheep.

**You write,** "It is not surprising that the largest churches in America are little more than entertaining social clubs with inspiring musical performances followed by the commercial messages of aspiring entrepreneurial preachers." **That's a pretty strong indictment. Do you really think large churches in America are social clubs that entertain?**

Yes, I think so. I'm troubled by that trend and wish that it weren't true. The drift toward entertainment has been progressively moving into congregations over the past 50 years and is related, I think, to two main developments. The first is a trend, evident throughout the past 50 years, where local churches have attempted to rescue falling attendance by making the church service itself more culturally "relevant." Churches found that they were competing with alternative activities including recreational and entertainment options that progressively eroded their weekly attendance. Their response was to try to out-entertain those options.

The second development is more recent. It is a similar response to the first but the impact has been much more profound. There is a disturbing trend toward what are now called "Mega-Churches." These churches attempt to create campuses that provide direct competition with local restaurants, movie theatres and fitness centers (just to name a few). The goal has been to entice both the discouraged believer and the unchurched into an environment where the Gospel is preached by cultural osmosis. The environment is designed to present an idyllic atmosphere resembling retreat centers. In some cases, the church becomes a "home away from home" but the end result is the encouragement of a "bunker mentality" where Christians hide from the world and where those who are only nominally "Christian" satisfy their own urges to belong to something seen as socially redeeming.

**Are you suggesting that the Gospel isn't preached in these Mega Churches?**

No, I'm not saying that. I'm saying that the Gospel is preached through cultural osmosis. The unchurched do hear sermons but those sermons are primarily directed toward making Christianity culturally relevant. Committed Christians receive nothing in these sermons that build up their theological base of knowledge. The effect is to culturally reform Christianity into a more palatable belief rather than theologically impacting and changing the culture around us.

**How about an example of what you're talking about?**

Great! Let's take music – church music – as the example. Scripture is clear that music did play a role even in the early church in Jerusalem and beyond. The early Christians definitely sang hymns, a few of which are included in Paul's epistles. The purpose of these hymns was to set doctrinal dogma to music so that it was more easily memorized. That practice continued throughout Church history until a uniquely American phenomenon occurred during the American revivals of the 20th Century. Revivals were "juiced up" by catchy and popular lyrics often set to the familiar pop tunes of the times.

Focus was then centered on various performers (soloists, ensembles and especially quartets) who performed Christian music and promoted their songs through commercially familiar channels or newly developed Christian "labels." I am not suggesting for a moment that these songs and the performers themselves weren't inspirational or that their lyrics weren't consistent with Christian theology. I am merely suggesting that the development has led local congregations to employ, in some cases, professional musicians and performers to "lead" congregational singing. I put "lead" in quotation marks because in many cases the congregation is not participating but merely watching a performance. This development should raise cautionary flags to all believers because the focus in these churches continues to move away from our Savior and his work in our lives and toward the skills, talents, personalities and entertainment value of human beings. The history of Christianity has demonstrated over and over that Christ must always be the center of our attention. The emergence of charismatic individuals often leads to forms of idolatry complete with personality cult-like fanaticism. One disturbing trend is that congregants, more than ever, change churches to follow charismatic preachers or other influential people. In doing so they are abandoning the fellowship they enjoyed with other believers and potentially leaving those without important comfort and care.

**People have always coalesced around charismatic leaders both within and without the Church. How does Christian theology address that?**

First of all, Christians need to be reminded (often it would seem) of just what the Sovereignty of God means. Among other things it means that God actively and proactively involves himself in our lives. That involvement, as promised by Jesus prior to his ascension, comes to us through God's Holy Spirit. God made us in his image and part of that image includes the emotional satisfaction humanity craves from relationships both with other humans and especially with God himself. Christians need to place greater faith in God's own personal intervention in their lives when it comes to inspiration. God can make us laugh, cry, feel and express the multitude of emotions that are uniquely human and divine. God, in short, is incredibly entertaining.

This is one of the central reasons Jesus taught his disciples two very important lessons. The first was not to take credit for the wonderful acts of God. When the disciples were sent out to heal the sick and cast out demons they returned to Jesus with justifiable excitement. They were excited to experience the fact that they were able to cast out demons in Jesus' name. Jesus told them not to rejoice over the fact that demons submitted to them but that their names were written in heaven. In others words we should be far more excited about our own personal salvation than by any other amazing personal achievement.

The second lesson was the lesson Jesus taught his disciples when he humbled himself and washed their feet prior to his last Passover meal with them. Christian leaders with cult-like followings really need to openly and actively live a life of humility and service toward others. They should not, in any way – even through omission – convey that their level of spirituality exceeds that of any other Christian.

**What are some of things that "ought" to happen in Christian church services that don't happen now?**

If there was one thing I would like to see happen in Christian Churches (Catholic and Protestant churches alike), it would be an open act of contrition on the part of all members, including the clergy, like that which happens at typical Alcoholics Anonymous meetings. It's been shown, though generally parodied, on television. An alcoholic stands up and says, "Hi, my name is Garry, and I'm an alcoholic." At once all the members in the group kindly say, "Hi, Garry."

I would like to see Christians promote that kind of humility inside and especially outside the church. Our theology clearly holds that all of humanity is sinful including ourselves. It is by grace that we have all been saved. So, I would love to see everyone that stands in front of a microphone during a service open with a statement like this: "Hi, I'm Garry and I'm a sinner."

I also want to point out that Christianity's more liturgical churches already have forms of this in their liturgy. Congregants, during responsive readings, often attest to their sinfulness. This may be, by the way, one of the reasons our more liturgical brethren find our more charismatic and spontaneous brethren somewhat "off-putting" in a self-righteous kind of way.

**Given the differences between denominations of Christianity can you suggest some practical ways Christians can begin a productive dialogue that leads to the "Promised Land" of a new American majority?**

I'm clearly hoping that my book will provide a foundation of *essential agreement* between the various denominations. But, I'm also sensitive to my own belief in not elevating myself (or my book) to a kind of "guru" status that I openly criticize in others. I don't want my book to be "peddled" over some kind of Christian shopping network. That being said, I would suggest that Christian leaders, in the clergy and the laity, begin a consistent drive toward their own biblical and theological literacy. American congregants who read or hear similar messages should do the same thing striving toward the goal of knowing when and how the sermons, or any religious message, they hear depart from the fundamental tenets of Christianity.

The dialogue itself will need a forum. It is my hope that a forum will emerge through the standard media. I believe God will make that happen and am waiting with anticipation to see his will be done.

**You wrote,** "While the country enjoys a relatively high level of literacy – the ability to read and write – our educational system is producing graduates who have no interest in or ability to produce cogent political or religious thought." **Are you referring to high school graduates or college graduates? When should someone be expected to be able to produce cogent political or religious thought?**

That's another great question and I'll answer it with a rhetorical question of my own. What is the voting age in America? The answer to that question clearly suggests that Americans ought to be able to carry on a cogent (that means internally consistent) argument supporting their political or religious beliefs before they step into a voting booth.

I also write about the fact that all rational thought ultimately rests on a final assumption that must be taken by faith. Our public school curriculums avoid discussions about faith as though it were a plague. Instead, teachers should be actively helping students identify their own faith (presuppositions) and then helping them to produce supporting rational arguments based on that faith – no matter what that faith may be. In the absence of this kind of rational thought students essentially learn to make political and religious decisions based exclusively on emotions or how they "feel" about a subject. Feelings lead to disruptive and emotion laden divisions in the America. That is one of the reasons Americans generally avoid discussions about religion or politics in mixed company. The discussions nearly always get emotional and too often end with everyone feeling angry and stressed out.

If voters of any age can identify the one underlying presupposition which they accept on faith, they can have productive dialogues that remain respectful and courteous toward those with whom they disagree. To prove my point try tuning into one of the many television programs where political pundits from the left and right square off in impromptu debate. These debates rarely begin with both sides acknowledging the other's fundamental presupposition that is based on their immoveable faith. The result is strident arguments that often lead to disrespectful attacks on the "intelligence" of the participants.

**You write that Christian theology supports capitalism as an economic system and you clearly state that capitalism should have reasonable restrictions that prohibit monopolies and encourage competition. Can you be more specific?**

I could be more specific but choose not to for one simple reason. It would be presumptuous for me to present a long list of restrictions on specific issues when I think those issues should be joined by the entire community of Christianity and the rest of the American populace for that matter. I hope it is sufficient to admit that a completely unfettered capitalism will produce inequities that Christians could not, in good conscience, support over the long term. Capitalism is great at harnessing something theologically "bad" (greed) and directing it toward something "good" for everyone (productivity). Restrictions on capitalism should be limited to those things which foster its good results while continuing to hold in check bad results.

**It seems like you have gone to great lengths to avoid identifying yourself with a political party in America. Why?**

Because, from a theological standpoint, America's two major political parties are both abject failures. My book retells the history of the Moral Majority and its rather obvious affiliation with the Republican Party to illustrate that while Christians can have a major impact on policy in general, its own policies will be diminished in value if they become merely a part of something larger and, by necessity, more diverse. Neither political party will ever consider themselves "the" party of Christianity. If they do that, they will chase important constituencies away and eliminate their chance to control a broad and sustainable base.

Christians do have options. They could abandon both parties in favor of establishing their own which, statistically, should be a majority. My fear is that a "Christian Party" would no doubt exhibit the same propensity as Democrats and Republicans to water down the message and broaden the tent beyond reason. That is, as pointed out in my book, the nature of humanity. It is flawed and all human organizations experience entropy (the breakdown of momentum) over time. I would personally like to see a political movement wherein Christians withhold affiliation and especially financial support from either party while instead throwing their blood, sweat, tears and money, to individual candidates who promise to support economic and political policies that are consistent with our theology.

Christians should also become more vocal in the media and call out those representatives who waiver on critical policies.

**Isn't it possible that an active and vocal Christian political movement will build resentment among non-Christians? That would not be a good thing, right?**

Christian theology would not support the restriction of freedoms expressly provided in America's current Constitution, its amendments and the Declaration of Independence. Christians, in fact, must work only within that framework to compel change in America's political policy. As clearly stated in my book, biblical theology does not support rebellion – even the one that started America.

Christians may not ever be able to keep an "us vs. them" mentality from emerging among non-Christians but they can, in every way imaginable, promote kindness in dialogue, respect for others, and loving service to everyone. Jesus told his disciples, "This is true religion, to care for widows and orphans." If Christians would only practice what they preach, there would be precious little for anyone to criticize in our character. They can, on the basis of their own theology, criticize our political objectives – that is an American right. They can and will vote their own consciences and Christians must always show proper respect for the conscience of others. Naturally, it is my hope that within the framework of our representative republic Christians will form a new majority that returns the nation to a sustainable future.

**Your book is about Christian theology and its impact on economics and politics but doesn't say much at all about religion other than it is just the practice of theology. What was your own "religious" background and how did it impact your life?**

I was raised in an Assembly of God church in Denver, Colorado under the leadership of two influential pastors. The first, Verne J. Crews, to my knowledge did not graduate from an accredited college but I would favorably compare him, in terms of biblical and theological literacy, with any one of my Seminary instructors (all PhD's). His preaching was "expository" meaning that he preached directly from Scripture, using Scripture to explain itself and taught an internally consistent theology (what scholars call biblical theology) even before the term was coined.

My second pastor was Eugene Gustafson, an exceedingly congenial man who was highly educated but was known most for his unique gifts of administration and service. He was an excellent counselor and provided wisdom in his sermons which were always quiet, rational and biblical. He was the opposite of the prototypical (perhaps stereotypical) Pentecostal preacher.

Having said that, the primary place I learned Scripture and its interpretation was in my home. My parents conducted daily family Bible reading and prayer every morning and my grandparents (whom I visited regularly) conducted Bible reading and prayer both morning and night. This practice was called the "family altar" because we were encouraged to pray for ourselves and for others in the Christian walk.

My father and mother were both gifted Bible students and lay teachers in my church. Neither were college educated; my mother had only an eighth grade education. Ours was a family that discussed the Bible's meaning often and, as you can imagine, religion and politics were not avoided – ever! On the contrary, my brothers, sisters and I almost always get around to a theological discussion at least once every time we get together to this day.

In terms of theology, I was raised as an evangelical with a non-Calvinist (Arminian) view of salvation. I accepted Jesus as the Son of God and my Savior when

I was just 5 years old. By the time I had graduated from high school I had probably read the entire Bible more than 10 times and individual books of the Bible hundreds of times but, more importantly, I took notes during sermons and often checked out ideas that I heard but thought perhaps inconsistent with Scripture. I carried my Bible with me at all times throughout high school but was never considered stuffy or legalistic toward others. Some of my best friends in high school were anything but Christian.

I went on to attend Evangel University (then Evangel College) which was and still is an Assembly of God denominational institution. There, I completed 16 hours of biblical study courses in addition to my major (Business Management) and a concentration in Social Science. I was active in student government and spent two summers working in youth ministry. After 26 years in private business pursuits, I returned to the Assembly of God denomination's Seminary to earn my Master's Degree in Theological Studies.

My theological views are not completely consistent with those held by the Assemblies of God as a denomination. I hold different views on a few issues but would nevertheless commend that denomination as a great place to grow in Christ and in the love of others. My work, as a writer and theologian, has motivated me to remain silent on some of the more contentious issues of doctrine and practice because, frankly, they won't matter very much when Jesus returns to straighten all of us out.

**You were raised a Protestant, attended a Protestant college and a Protestant Seminary. What about Catholicism? Do you have any words for Catholics?**

All of Christianity grew out of the Catholic Church and Christianity in total owes a great debt of gratitude to the Catholic Church for its preservation of Scripture and for its protection of Christian theological orthodoxy. Everyone knows that the Reformation was a movement in response to the spiritual and doctrinal decline of Christianity as expressed in the mediaeval Church. Notwithstanding all of that, the fundamental theological basis of Christianity remains consistent between Catholic and Protestant.

The most dramatic differences, theologically, are beliefs surrounding the biblical teaching of the Eucharist (the Lord's Supper or Communion) and the role of Mary, Jesus' mother, in terms of her character and divinely appointed role as the mother of Jesus or, as Catholics call her, the Mother of God. All other differences are less doctrinal and more matters of practice. For example, the Catholic Church believes that church polity (its leadership) must be vested in the progressive apostolic succession. Priests are appointed, not elected, and are ultimately accountable, as are all Catholics, to the Pope who is in a more or less unbroken apostolic succession dating back to the Apostle Peter. Protestants and Catholics can certainly agree to disagree on an issue like that and still remain in fundamental fellowship based on the common theology that Jesus is the Son of God, who died on the cross as a substitutional sacrifice for all of humanity's sins, etc.

182

On the most fundamental of all theologically based political policies – abortion – the two could not be in more agreement. I would hope, in fact, that a new American majority of Christians would include all those who are called by his name.

**Biblical prophecy seems, especially in Revelation, to point to a time when the Church will be unified but also Apostate or fallen in the corruption of an "Anti-Christ." Aren't you afraid that bringing all Christians together for "politics" will just hasten that development?**

A great cake requires that great ingredients are mixed together and baked. After it is baked, it ought to be eaten because in spite of its great ingredients it will certainly rot over time. The Church Universal (which is this case means the entire Body of Christ – worldwide) is like that cake. If we put all of the ingredients together and bake it, we will all smell the wonderful aroma of its essence. However, that cake is meant to be eaten or, in this simile, consumed by the world of unbelievers. That portion that is not consumed will definitely rot.

At some point in the last days the Church will be taken away to be with Christ in what is sometimes called the rapture. Those left behind will no doubt include some who may have been in our cake but weren't consumed by the world. Those who remain here on earth during what is commonly called the Great Tribulation will certainly have to choose whether they remain in an Apostate Church or allow themselves to finally be consumed in the persecution that is prophesied.

**You mentioned something a bit weird but actually funny in your book about baseball's designated hitter rule being one example of a change made because of America's drive for immediate gratification. Are you serious?**

Yes, and I'll stake my theological reputation on the belief that there are no designated hitters in heaven. As a former college baseball player (who, by the way sat on the bench 95% of the time) I would have cried if someone else was allowed to bat for me because it was one of those incorruptible truths that if you play in the field, you *get* to bat. Taking that away is like God telling all the Christian preachers in this world that they have to *pitch* his theology all of their lives here but don't get to go to heaven because he has designated heaven goers instead. Long live the National League!

**This book defies a singular description in terms of where it would be displayed in a bookstore. It covers theology, economics, politics and religion. Where would you put it in a Barnes & Noble or a Borders bookstore?**

You're right! It has to go in the very front of the store on its own display.

**It appears logical that this book is intended for Christians. Since you are clearly against churches selling books and tapes in the foyer, how do you intend to sell this book?**

Like all evangelicals I don't think my own rules apply to me so I'm going to put it right back there with all the other materials on sale here. Just kidding!

I sincerely hope first of all that people, Christians and non-Christians, will want to buy my book. It will eventually be available at major bookstores but one might have to place an order because no writer can be assured that a book will sell widely enough for a mainline bookstore to stock it.

The initial publication of my book was self-funded and "self-published." That means that, like a good capitalist, I invested the time and energy to produce it without any guarantee that it would be commercially viable. Those interested can order it from my website and whenever I speak at a church the book will be sold (like any other aspiring writer) from the trunk of my car outside in the parking lot.

In any case, I am very serious about my belief that churches need to refrain from commercial activities that should be accomplished by for-profit private or public companies.

Visit my website at www.faithpolicy.com

www.ingramcontent.com/pod-product-compliance
Lightning Source LLC
LaVergne TN
LVHW051632080426
835511LV00016B/2317